Christian Ministry in the Divine Milieu

D1069417

Catholicity in an Evolving Universe
Ilia Delio, General Editor

This series of original works by leading Catholic figures explores all facets of life through the lens of catholicity: a sense of dynamic wholeness and a conscious awareness of a continually unfolding creation.

Christian Ministry in the Divine Milieu

Catholicity, Evolution, and the Reign of God

DONALD C. MALDARI, SJ

ORBIS BOOKS

Maryknoll, New York 10545

Founded in 1970, Orbis Books endeavors to publish works that enlighten the mind, nourish the spirit, and challenge the conscience. The publishing arm of the Maryknoll Fathers and Brothers, Orbis seeks to explore the global dimensions of the Christian faith and mission, to invite dialogue with diverse cultures and religious traditions, and to serve the cause of reconciliation and peace. The books published reflect the views of their authors and do not represent the official position of the Maryknoll Society. To learn more about Maryknoll and Orbis Books, please visit our website at www.maryknollsociety.org.

Manufactured in the United States of America.
Manuscript editing and typesetting by Joan Weber Laflamme.

Library of Congress Cataloging-in-Publication Data

Names: Maldari, Donald C., author.
Title: Christian ministry in the divine milieu : Catholicity, evolution, and the reign of God / Donald C. Maldari, SJ.
Description: Maryknoll : Orbis Books, 2019. | Series: Catholicity in an evolving universe | Includes bibliographical references and index.
Identifiers: LCCN 2018035115 (print) | LCCN 2018052687 (ebook) | ISBN 9781608337743 (ebook) | ISBN 9781626983137 (pbk.)
Subjects: LCSH: Priesthood—Catholic Church. | Pastoral theology—Catholic Church. | Church work—Catholic Church.
Classification: LCC BX1913 (ebook) | LCC BX1913 .M325 2019 (print) | DDC 262/.142—dc23
LC record available at https://lccn.loc.gov/2018035115

Contents

Acknowledgments

I was first introduced to the thought of Pierre Teilhard de Chardin in a theology course that I took with Rev. Thomas King, SJ, as an undergraduate at Georgetown University. The semester before, I took a course in physics, and soon after, one in chemistry. Alas, it took several decades for me to make the connection among those three courses. Once I did, I began to marvel at the unity and catholicity of all that exists. I am very grateful to Tom King for planting the Teilhardian seed.

Thanks go out to Ilia Delio, Mary Evelyn Tucker, Brother Jeffrey Gros, and David Grumett for organizing the 2010 conference at Santa Clara University entitled Pierre Teilhard de Chardin for a New Generation. The papers and interactions served to stimulate my reflection on the connections between theology and science to which I had been introduced so many years earlier.

I am also grateful to Joseph F. Wimmer, OSA, and Daryl P. Domning, PhD, for organizing the riveting series of conferences at the Washington Theological Union from 2011 to 2013 with the clever title The Atom and Eve Project. The papers presented at those conferences mesmerized me and inspired me to pursue research into the relationship between theology and the sciences. I am particularly grateful for my correspondence with Daryl Domning after the conferences. His insightful book *Original Selfishness: Original Sin and Evil in Light of Evolution*, co-authored by another one of my inspirational professors at Georgetown, Monika Hellwig, has not only influenced this book but also any number of courses that I have taught over the years. The work of Martin Nowak, professor of biology and mathematics and director of the Program for Evolutionary Dynamics at Harvard University, has been pivotal in the development of my thought.

George V. Coyne, SJ, former director of the Vatican Observatory and currently the holder of a McDevitt Chair at Le Moyne College in Syracuse, New York, has been of invaluable help, especially in aiding me to navigate the rudiments of physics. I learned a great deal from him in the course we taught together at Le Moyne College, Religion and Science, and I am forever grateful for his careful reading of my first book and the bits about physics in this one.

Many thanks to Le Moyne College for supporting my research with the Fallon Endowed Chair. Thanks also to my colleagues at the Pacific Regional Seminary in Suva, Fiji, for their encouragement and support. I am deeply grateful to my students at both Le Moyne College and at the Pacific Regional Seminary. Discussions with them in and out of the classroom have stimulated my thought.

Finally, thanks to the parishioners of Immaculate Heart of Mary and St. Joseph the Worker parishes in Liverpool, New York, for reminding me how the theories of theology are received and lived among the people of God.

Foreword

Ilia Delio

Physicists today are recognizing the fundamental role of consciousness in the formation of physical reality. Some scientists suggest that we live in a top-down or holist universe, in which complex wholes are more fundamental than their parts. A holistic paradigm means that everything that exists derives its existence from the ultimate complex system, the universe as a whole. When holism is combined with the universality of consciousness or panpsychism, one arrives at the notion that the universe is conscious and that the consciousness of everything that exists is derived not from the consciousness of fundamental particles but the consciousness of the universe itself.

When we translate these scientific ideas into the framework of catholicity and ministry in an evolving world, we come to the essence of Donald Maldari's book. Using the insights of Teilhard de Chardin and his notion of the divine milieu, Maldari explores ministry as a function of catholicity, that is, a consciousness of belonging to a whole—the body of Christ—which, as Teilhard wrote, is in evolution.

Father Maldari nicely situates catholicity in evolution as the rise of consciousness and the emergence of religion. Ralph Wendell Burhoe wrote that religion "is the key and hitherto missing link in the scientific explanation of how ape-men are transformed to civilized altruism." We have evolved to be "religious" in the sense that we have the possibility of organizing our lives, our activities, in function of what we perceive as our ultimate goal; that is, religion emerges with higher levels of consciousness.

Catholicity is the awareness of belonging to a whole and acting on behalf of the whole, a key idea in Maldari's work. Avery Dulles spoke of catholicity as "a divine gift and a human task." The divine gift is the trinitarian outflow of love, and our task is to abandon our individualism, our selfishness, and our instinct to compete in order to work cooperatively. A higher consciousness of belonging to a whole grounded in the love of God means that competition and individualism must give way to cooperation and community. The sacrament of baptism that initiates one into the church involves death to the old order of natural selection, including selfishness and competition, and rebirth into the new order of pure altruism and cooperation; baptism is the call to community.

Catholicity undergirds the movement toward unity by emphasizing the contributions of each member of the community. Maldari explores this idea through the writings of Vatican II, scientific findings, and the work of religious scholars. By engaging a consciousness of ministry in evolution, we begin to realize our task as created co-creators, called to participate with God in the unfolding of a new world grounded in Christ, a "kin-dom" of interdependence and fecund life. To minister on behalf of the church, therefore, is not simply to work but to serve; not to accomplish but to participate. We have lost sight of ministry as a participation in the whole, the Christ in evolution, and have reduced ministry to particular jobs in the church. We have failed to let go of these jobs at times because we do not have a sense of being in evolution. Systems specialist Eric Jantsch writes, "To live with an evolutionary spirit is to let go when the right time comes and to engage new structures of relationships." This letting-go process is reflective of systems-thinking rather than individualism. An individual approach to ministry reflects a metaphysics of substance and eternal presence. Dulles said that "just as in early modern times Catholics tended to confuse universality with uniformity, so they tended to equate continuity with immutability." A church immune to change, however, is a church bound for extinction. However, the church can flourish if it adapts to the dynamic principles of evolution: novelty, creativity, and a future orientation. In this respect the requirement of a permanent commitment to a particular ministry seems unnecessary, according to Maldari, and, in light of the inherent flexibility of catholicity, perhaps even unwise. The Christian *religio*, bound to and guided by the whole of Christ, must adapt to the times by expressing the same faith in different ways. The church's catholicity would be better served if people were able to discern the present needs and change the type of service they contribute to the community. God has not gone away but is showing up in new places, and one who ministers on behalf of the church must be attentive to the new areas where God is shining through.

Father Maldari's book is a welcome addition to the catholicity series because it opens up a conversation on church and evolution in a way that Pope Francis is trying to do as well. To be attentive to the signs of the time is to live on the threshold of the future; that is, to be ready to engage the new because life is evolving in creative ways. God is not retired; God *is* doing new things.

Introduction

We human beings are a very active bunch. A good portion of our youth, especially, is spent figuring out what kinds of activities we want to be engaged in. We feel a variety of calls or inclinations regarding our future, and we expend a great deal of energy trying to figure out what those calls mean. What do we want to *do* with our lives? we ask. As we pursue the answer to this question it dawns on us that we need some clarity on another question first: Who do I want to *be*? Who I *am* depends to a large degree on what I *do,* and what I *do* depends to a large degree on who I *am.*

Christians characterize the calls to do and to be as vocations: What is God calling me to do? Who is God calling me to be? Christians have a pretty simple yet profound answer to the second question: We are called to be participants in the community that is God. We are called to salvation. We are called to holiness. We are called to be saints. Ancient Christians referred to this call as *deification.* The second-century church father Irenaeus of Lyons expresses what a good many other ancient Christian writers also wrote: God "made himself what we are, that he might bring us to be even what he is himself."[1] The answer to the second question—What is God calling me to do?—flows from the answer to the first one. What people ought to *do* is to work on becoming who we *are.*

---

[1] *Adversus haereses*, book 5, preface: "Factus est quod sumus nos, uti nos perficeret quod et ipse."

The Context
of Our Consideration of Ministry

Everything that we do takes place in the finite universe that Christians call creation. Paleontologist Pierre Teilhard de Chardin, using the lens of faith to understand what he learned about the universe through reason, characterized the universe as the divine milieu. Teilhard demonstrated that reason and faith, science and theology, are not at all contradictory but complementary. Teilhard's work in the natural sciences, using reason alone, helped him better to understand how the world works. But he was not satisfied with answers of only *how, when, where,* and *what* with respect to the world. He also wanted to know *why* the world exists in general and why we humans exist in particular. Knowing *why* we exist sheds light on what we should *do.*

Our study of the catholicity of ministry will begin by using reason to look at the storyline of the universe. We will take a look at what the natural and social sciences can tell us about *how* the universe in general and people in particular work in order to move to a consideration through faith of *why* the universe works. Insight into the *how* of the universe will offer us insight into the *why* of the universe and, in particular, the *why* of people. We will see that the study of *how* God creates is characterized by as-yet-unanswered questions, such as black holes, dark matter, maybe even alternate universes. Science cannot appeal to mystery; in the immanent dimension of reality there are only things that we do not understand . . . yet. We just need more time, data, and lots of smarts. The study of *why* God creates and of the ultimate goal of salvation, on the other hand, most definitely does involve mystery. God's will surpasses our human ability to understand. God is infinite; our brains are finite. We can no more fully understand God than we can put the entire ocean into a thimble. But by studying the water in the thimble we can know something about the ocean.

In order to consider why we are here, and what we should be doing to fulfill that why, we will situate human work in the context of what we know from science: the laws of thermodynamics, Darwin's theory of evolution, and social studies on the human instinct toward cooperation. We'll do so because we are integral parts of the universe that God is creating. From thermodynamics we'll see how we, like everything in the universe, consist of energy and matter, and how energy works on matter. From evolution we'll see the trajectory and patterns of development in the universe, of which we are a product. Finally, studies in social behavior will reveal how we construct our relationships with one another in this great process of evolution. Knowing how we fit into the universe will help us turn our eyes of faith upon these phenomena in order to perceive and reflect upon God's creative process. We can in this way better understand how we can work fruitfully with God and recognize the activities in which we engage that frustrate the divine plan—what theologians call sin.

After considering *how* we fit into the universe we'll move on to consider *why* we fit into the universe. What is our purpose and role? This is a question not for the natural and social sciences but for theology, that is, faith seeking understanding. In one of the mystical experiences that Saint Augustine describes in *The Confessions*, Augustine, like Teilhard centuries later, recognizes the complementary relationship between reason and faith in the human quest to respond to our vocations. Augustine recounts that his use of reason in trying to satisfy his thirst for truth took him a long way toward his goal. Reason alone, however, was insufficient; he had to resort to faith to go beyond the limits of reason.

Teilhard learned from Augustine. He looked at the data he studied through reason in the natural sciences through the lens of faith and he saw that all creation is being called to participate in the communion that is God. Inspired by the spirituality of the founder of his order, Ignatius Loyola, he saw the Trinity at work in the Son through whom the Father creates by the power of the Holy Spirit.[2] Teilhard saw that the universe is

---

[2] See Rogelio García Mateo, SJ, "'Criador y Redentor Nuestro': La Misión del Hijo según Ignacio de Loyola," *Estudios Eclesiásticos* 90 (2015): 569–91; Kathleen Duffy, SSJ, "The Spiritual Power of Matter: Teilhard and the 'Exercises,'" *Review for Religious* 63 (2004): 192–203.

a divine milieu. He perceived the presence of the triune God through the incarnate Son in all things, working together for the good, especially and most fully in Jesus. He showed us that our universe is the continuing creative act of God. God works through the nature that God created, including humans. God respects the laws of nature that God made and so, say theologians, God works through creation. Human work that advances God's creative act participates in that creative act and, indeed, is essential to that creative act. Why? Because that's the way God set it up!

The complementarity of reason and faith in the human search to understand the meaning of the universe involves the recognition of the unity of reality and of at least two dimensions of reality. One dimension is the *immanent*. This is the dimension that we know through the use of reason. This is the "stuff" of everyday life that we perceive with our natural senses and think about: things that we taste, smell, touch, hear, and see. This is the dimension of reality that scientists study.

Another dimension of reality is the *transcendent*. This is the dimension we know through the use of faith. Through our knowledge of the immanent dimension by the use of reason we can, with the willing suspension of disbelief, see the transcendent dimension.[3] We know this dimension through visual and performing art, literature, and music. It's the beauty that we perceive when gazing at a rainbow or a flower. It's the moral wrong that we recognize in injustice. In 1670, Blaise Pascal warned of the rejection of faith in favor of reason when he wrote: "The heart has reasons of which reason knows nothing."[4] Reason alone cannot understand all of reality. Reason alone cannot know love. Reason alone cannot know God.

---

[3] The expression "willing suspension of disbelief" was coined by the English poet Samuel Taylor Coleridge in *Biographia Literaria* (London: Rest Fenner, 1817) as a plea for people who thought they could know everything by the use of reason alone.

[4] Blaise Pascal, *Pensées* 277: "Le coeur a ses raisons que la raison ne connaît point."

The Illegitimate Division between Secular and Sacred

Twenty-first-century culture that is influenced by Western thought has a tendency to understand the immanent and transcendent not as two dimensions of reality but rather as two different realities. It also often either rejects the existence of the transcendent or it restricts it to what is commonly called religion. It introduces an artificial dualism into how we understand reality. The immanent dimension is too often considered to be the only *real* dimension. This split between the immanent and transcendent also splits how we understand ourselves and the value of our work. It's an ironic twist on a preceding split in Western thought between the natural and the supernatural. In this split the natural was thought of as only transitory. The only meaning human activity had, besides prayer, was just to stay alive and, depending on one's Christian affiliation, please God. The supernatural, that is, heaven, on the other hand, was what really counted. Adapting Plato's dualism of a transitory body and the eternity of a spiritual afterlife, Christians looked forward to a death that would liberate them from this vale of tears. Here human work had little meaning.

What made Western European culture flip its understanding of reality? Well, a funny thing happened in Europe on the way to the eighteenth century: the Enlightenment. The Enlightenment, also known as the Age of Reason, radically changed how Westerners thought about life and human culture. The change came in the wake of the so-called Wars of Religion following the Protestant Reformation and the church's intolerance of scientists and philosophers in the fifteenth to seventeenth centuries. Church authorities condemned these thinkers when their ideas or discoveries contradicted what people had accepted as divine revelation, including the split between body and soul. By the eighteenth century many thinkers were fed up with what amounted to the church's fundamentalist approach to knowledge. They decided to separate people's faith in a transcendent ultimate meaning from people's lives in the immanent dimension of reality, but instead of valuing the transcendent over the immanent, they valued the immanent over the transcendent. They also either questioned or rejected the value of faith in the human quest for knowledge.

One of the innovations that eighteenth-century thinkers introduced into Western thought, especially on the part of those in France known as the Encyclopedists, was the redefinition of the word *religion*.[5] Before the Enlightenment *religion* retained a reference to its root in Latin: *religio*. *Religio* referred to people's obligation to God, including shaping themselves and their entire cultures in function of their relationship with their God or gods.[6] Before the Enlightenment, *religio* took for granted the unity of the immanent and transcendent dimensions of reality, even if one was more important than the other. It valued knowledge attained by both reason and faith. Enlightenment thinkers divided those dimensions as if they were two different realities and questioned whether the transcendent had anything to do with reality at all. The immanent dimension of reality was identified as profane and secular; the transcendent, if it existed, as sacred and religious. Those thinkers did so because they discounted the validity of knowledge attained through faith. They were "enlightened" after humanity had lived so long in the darkness imposed by faith. The fundamentalist attitude of the eighteenth-century church had made faith appear unreasonable—a betrayal of the great tradition of the medieval universities founded by that same church.

As a result of the devaluation of faith in Western cultures, these cultures began simply to ignore the transcendent dimension of reality or relegate it to the museum of ancient history. After

---

[5] See Michel Despland, *La religion en occident: Évolution des idées et du vécu. Mythes, sciences et idéologie (Les Dieux dans la Cité. Religions et Sociétés)* (Montreal: Les Éditions Fides, 1979); Daniel Dubuisson, *L'Occident et la religion* (Brussels: Éditions complexe, 1998); Wilfred Cantwell Smith, *The Meaning and End of Religion* (Minneapolis: Fortress Press, 1963); William T. Cavanaugh, *The Myth of Religious Violence: Secular Ideology and the Roots of Modern Conflict* (Oxford: Oxford University Press, 2009), esp. 57–122; William Irons, "An Inquiry into the Evolutionary Origin of Religion," *Currents in Theology and Mission* 28 (2001): 357–68; Peter Sloterdijk, *You Must Change Your Life,* trans. Wieland Hoban (Cambridge: Polity Press, 2013).

[6] Brent Nongbri, *Before Religion: A History of a Concept* (New Haven, CT: Yale University Press, 2013); Carlin A. Barton and Daniel Boyarin, *Imagine No Religion: How Modern Abstractions Hide Ancient Realities* (New York: Fordham University Press, 2016).

the French Revolution religion was banned from participation in the public arena. A woman representing the Goddess of Reason stood on the high altar of the Cathedral of Notre-Dame in Paris to indicate that reason had replaced faith as the means of knowing all truth.[7] The use of some form of the French word *laïcité* (secularism) to ensure that culture develops free of any reference to God is a modern manifestation of this same mindset.

Modern Westerners are often incredulous to learn that the separation of the two dimensions of reality, and the subsequent redefinition of religion, is actually unique to themselves. No other culture on earth has an equivalent indigenous word or concept that corresponds to the post-Enlightenment understanding of religion.[8] Secularization is the West's gift to the rest of the world.

Since the dawn of secularization the church and everything about it has been understood as separate from the state, politics, business, the economy, and so forth. People identify the world with reason, the church with faith. It's an easy jump to see how people understand the work they do in the world as governed only by reason. We understand everyday work as a secular enterprise, independent from people's faith. The work that people do in church has a special name: ministry. Ministry is religious; it deals only with our relationship with the transcendent. In the common mindset of the everyday, secular work is not ministry. We do not often see a connection between the work that we do outside of church, that is, our jobs and careers, and our relationship with God or the promotion of creation's fulfillment. We spend most of our waking hours either working or recovering from working with little if any

---

[7] See Mona Ozouf, *La fête révolutionnaire, 1789–1799* (Paris: Gallimard, 1976).

[8] Timothy Fitzpatrick, "A Critique of Religion as a Cross-Cultural Category," *Method and Theory in the Study of Religion* 9 (1997): 91–110; idem, *The Ideology of Religious Studies* (New York: Oxford University Press, 2000); idem, *Discourse on Civility and Barbarity: A Critical History of Religion and Related Categories* (New York: Oxford University Press, 2007); Werner Cohn, "Is Religion Universal? Problems of Definition," *Journal for the Scientific Study of Religion* 2 (1962): 25–35.

understanding of work's role in the cosmic order of things. We seem to ignore the fact that everything we do in the so-called secular milieu affects the divine milieu. Everything we do in creation either promotes or inhibits its evolution toward salvation.

Christians cannot accept this dualism between faith and reason, between the secular and the religious, the sacred and the profane. Christians use both reason and faith in order to understand the one reality of our world and our role in it. As Pope John Paul II writes in the introductory blessing of his encyclical *Fides et ratio*: "Faith and reason are like two wings on which the human spirit rises to the contemplation of truth; and God has placed in the human heart a desire to know the truth—in a word, to know himself—so that, by knowing and loving God, men and women may also come to the fullness of truth about themselves." What we discover by applying this method is that the universe is evolving because of the synergistic presence and work of the triune God in creation, each divine person expressing its own personality in unison with the whole of God.

The Christian understanding of reality, therefore, cannot separate the transcendent dimension from the immanent dimension. Reason perceives unity in the immanent dimension of reality. Physicists propose that all parts of the universe affect the rest of the universe because everything is connected. They illustrate this unity in what they playfully call the "butterfly effect." The butterfly effect goes like this: One single butterfly moving its wings in Australia moves the air that causes an ever-so-slight wind current. That wind current joins with other wind currents that are moved by a myriad of other causes. The wind blows across the planet, forming into a minor whirlwind. The whirlwind becomes more organized as more energy is pumped into it by heat rising from the ocean. That heat, of course, came from the sun and from heat trapped inside the planet. The whirlwind develops into a cyclone that passes over land masses, making life very difficult for other butterflies but also transferring heat from hot places to cool places. This transfer of heat is essential for the earth's ecosystem, including people. We owe our lives, at least in part, to that Australian butterfly.

The Christian Cosmology of Human Work

The principle behind the butterfly effect—that is, that everything is connected to everything else and affects everything else—applies to the whole universe. Faith reflects upon the data and theories of science; it perceives the unity of all reality, in both its immanent and transcendent dimensions. Christianity expresses that unity in both scripture and tradition. Both the Old and New Testaments repeatedly affirm their belief that God is one and that God permeates all of creation. The ancient formulations of Christian faith, the creeds, likewise proclaim the belief in one God. If God, the creator, is one, and God permeates all of reality, then all of creation is one reality.

Along with the Christian belief in God's unity is the belief in God's diversity. Reason perceives the diversity in the universe in the myriad particles that constitute it. In a mind-boggling cosmic dance these particles retain some sort of individuality while also forming the whole of the universe. They change constantly as they relate to other particles. The universe is therefore in constant flux yet remains the same universe. Faith again reflects upon the data and theories of science, and again it perceives the diversity of the universe in both its immanent and transcendent dimensions. Looking at the Old Testament through the lens of the revelation of the New Testament, Christian theology affirms its belief in the diversity of God. God is a holy trinity. God is three persons, for lack of a better word, whose existence is relational. In the Book of Genesis, God the Father creates through the Word he speaks by the power of the Spirit who hovers over the waters of creation. The Father is Father because of the relationship with the Son. There is no parent without a child. The Son is Son because of the relationship with the Father. There is no child without parents. The Spirit is the love that flows from the Father to the Son and back to the Father. Each has a different role in the constitution of the very being that is God. Each is essential; each is fully God; each has a defined role. Each person plays a distinct role in the divine act of creation. All the persons live and work together in what the ancient Christians called *perichoresis:* a relationship akin to a kind of divine, eternal dance.

Christianity sees God, who is diverse in three persons and unified in being, reflected in the universe that God is in the process of creating. Just as God is one, so is reality; just as God is diverse, so is reality. Everything in the universe is interconnected without losing its individuality. The universe is both stable and dynamic, ever the same and ever changing. Everything works together. God permeates every nook and cranny of the universe. God is dynamically present in all creation. Christianity sees that dynamism in the universe's evolution, growing toward a denouement. In the words of Saint Paul in his Letter to the Romans:

> We know that the whole creation has been groaning in labor pains until now; and not only the creation, but we ourselves, who have the first fruits of the Spirit, groan inwardly while we wait for adoption, the redemption of our bodies. . . . We know that all things work together for good for those who love God, who are called according to his purpose. (Rom 8:22–23, 28)

The unity and diversity that is God and that characterizes all creation is what we will call *catholicity*.

Catholicity

The words *catholicity* and *catholic* may cause confusion and need clarification. When we come across these words, they are often capitalized, and in common usage they usually refer to the church that is in union with the bishop of Rome. This is not how we are using the words here. Their association with the Church of Rome is, of course, a historically correct use of these words, but that usage is itself derived from a much earlier and broader definition. The word is actually derived from the ancient Greek word *katholikós*, which means "in general" or "universal." Christian theology adopted it to describe one of the characteristics or "notes" of the church. The creed formula promulgated by the Council of Constantinople in 381 thus describes the church as one, holy, catholic, and apostolic. The use of *katholikós* was a daring move by the council because it is the only one of the four adjectives that is not derived from the Bible. We know that the members of the council tried very hard to use biblical vocabulary that would be acceptable to a variety of dissonant if not feuding factions within the church at the time. The members of the council were no doubt still smarting from the infelicitous repercussions following the use of the nonbiblical word *homooúsios* at the Council of Nicaea fifty-six years earlier, in 325, which tried to resolve the Arian controversy. No one, however, seems to have objected to the equally nonbiblical word *katholikós*. Its choice was bold, deliberate, and popular.

Christian thought about the meaning of *katholikós* or "catholic" with reference to the church has evolved over the centuries. A constant, however, has been the desire to understand the one church as characterized by diverse people, customs, and talents.[9] This diversity reflects and participates in the very diversity that characterizes the life of the Trinity. Just as God's being is catholic, so is that of the church. Just as God's work is catholic, so is that of the church. Cardinal Walter Kasper relates the concept of catholicity to ministry in this way:

> Thus the [Second Vatican] Council was able to designate catholicity as a gift from the Lord, which as a gift at the same time represents a constantly renewed responsibility. Catholicity is to be understood as the involvement of all individuals, the various ministries and offices, all church bodies and peoples, collectively contributing their gifts

---

[9] See Gustave Thils, "La Notion de Catholicité de l'Église à l'Époque Moderne," *Ephemerides Theologicae Lovanienses* 13 (1936): 5–73; J.N.D. Kelly, "'Catholic' and 'Apostolic' in the Early Centuries," *One in Christ* 6 (1970): 274–87; Avery Dulles, SJ, *The Catholicity of the Church* (Oxford: Oxford University Press, 1985); Wolfgang Beinert, "Catholicity as a Property of the Church," *The Jurist* 52 (1992): 455–83; Vittorino Grossi, "Nota sobre la Semántica de la expresión 'Iglesia Católica antes y después del 'Edicto' de Constantino del 313," *Anuario de Historia de la Iglesia* 22 (2013): 111–33.

under the one head, Christ. Accordingly, catholicity is understood as a dynamic unity in diversity (cf. LG 13, 32).[10]

The Catholicity of Ministry

The church has applied the principle of catholicity to ministry in such a way that ministry has taken a large variety of forms over the centuries. It has done so in evolving cultures in different places. This makes perfect sense, as everything in creation, which includes the church, adapts to its evolving environment or dies. Furthermore, there is no indication whatever that Jesus intended ministry to take only one form in the church.[11] First of all, it is highly questionable if Jesus himself ever foresaw a church developing from his ministry. Only the Gospel of Matthew uses the word *ekklesía* (church), and those references are projections back onto the historical Jesus from the distance of several decades. The New Testament gives witness to a variety of ways by which the church organized itself. Importantly, the distinction between clergy and laity was unknown in the New Testament and probably into the early second century.[12] In the

---

[10] Walter Kasper, "'Credo Unam Sanctam Ecclesiam'—The Relationship Between the Catholic and the Protestant Principles in Fundamental Ecclesiology," *Receptive Ecumenism and the Call to Catholic Learning: Exploring a Way for Contemporary Ecumenism,* ed. P. D. Murray and Luca Badini Confalonieri (Oxford: Oxford University Press, 2008), 77–88. First published in the *International Journal for the Study of the Christian Church* 7 (2007): 250–60.

[11] See, for example, Juan Luis Segundo, SJ, "Did Christ Want Sacraments?" in *The Sacraments Today* (Maryknoll, NY: Orbis Books, 1974), 21–41; Bastiaan van Iersel, SMM, "Some Biblical Roots of the Christian Sacrament," Concilium, vol. 31, *Sacraments in General: A New Perspective,* ed. Edward Schillebeeckx, OP, and Boniface Willems, OP (New York: Paulist Press, 1968), 5–20; Bernard Cooke and Gary Macy, *Christian Symbol and Ritual: An Introduction* (New York: Oxford University Press, 2005).

[12] Alexandre Faivre, *Les premiers laïcs, lorsque l'Église naissait au monde* (Strasbourg: Édition du Signe 1999); idem, *Ordonner la fraternité. Pouvoir d'innover et retour à l'ordre dans l'Église ancienne* (Paris: Cerf, 1992).

age before religion became a subset of culture, Westerners, like everyone else in the world, understood everything that they did as possible contributions to the salvation or fulfillment of the community. People took on roles in the community depending on their personal talents. The community sanctioned those roles and commissioned those who undertook them with a ritual, recognizing that the work was being done for the good of the community. There is no reason not to think of those roles as ministry. In the early Christian church those who had talents to perform ritual and cultic activities were commissioned to do so, but the New Testament never singles them out for special mention. Anyone could baptize, and the New Testament never tells us who presided at the Eucharist. All members of the community contributed what they could to the life of the community and received what they needed for life from the community (Acts 4:32–37). The synergistic interconnectedness of those diverse ministries in the one church was and is catholic.

Human work in creation plays a crucial role in the process of creation. Teilhard wrote that grace divinizes our actions, promoting our communion with God and with one another. We harness the energy of the universe through our catholic work that is done in and through Jesus Christ. We are integral parts of the universe. We participate in God's creative activity through which, to use Saint Paul's image, creation is being born into its fulfillment. We participate, if inchoately right now, in the life of God. Just as the three persons of the Trinity relate to one another and work together in *perichoresis,* so humans do as well. Humanity is at once one and consists of many. The Book of Genesis recognizes us as the image and likeness of God.[13]

Genesis understands the human affinity with God as implying the human participation in, and promotion of, God's act of creation. We are, in the words of theologian Philip Hefner, "created co-creators."[14] Genesis sees us as blessed by God to "be fruitful and multiply, and fill the earth and subdue it; and

---

[13] See Anna Case-Winters, "Rethinking the Image of God," *Zygon* 39 (2004): 813–26.

[14] Philip Hefner, "Biocultural Evolution and the Created Co-Creator," *Dialog* 36 (1997): 197–205.

have dominion over . . . every living thing that moves upon the earth" (Gen 1:28). Scripture scholars understand the "subduing" and "dominion" to refer to our responsibility to direct creation to fulfillment. The New Testament describes us as participating in and continuing the work of Christ empowered by the Holy Spirit; we are charged to baptize all people into the Trinity (Matt 28:19), we are sent by Christ to continue his work of drawing creation to fulfillment just as he was sent by the Father (John 20:21), and we are charged to bring all people together in the church (Acts 2; Paul's understanding of the church as the body of Christ in his letters).

Life, as we all know at some level, culminates in death. Most creatures, as far as we can tell, remain blissfully ignorant of their inevitable death. We humans are not among them, even if we choose to ignore the inevitable. When we are honest with ourselves, we ask what the point of all our activity is. We wonder why we live if we're going to die. What's the point of working so hard? Does life have any meaning, or is it just absurd?

People have been asking these questions for as long as there have been people. The resounding consensus in human cultures throughout time and space is that life and work do have meaning. There is an insight that death is not the end and that what people do has an effect on who or what we become. We arrive at this insight by going beyond the data that the natural sciences alone provide. Through the eyes of faith we recognize the value of everything that people do—every activity, every job, every ritual, every project—either promotes what we perceive as our ultimate goal or hinders it. There are no exceptions to what is included in the mix.

Teilhard also expounds on the importance of joining Christ in his death as we approach our own individual death and that of the universe. Activity evolves into passivity. Teilhard muses about the human condition: "Having been perhaps primarily alive to the attractions of union with God through action, he begins to conceive and then to desire a complementary aspect, an ulterior phase, in his communion: one in which he would not develop himself so much as lose himself in God."[15] Death

---

[15] Pierre Teilhard de Chardin, *The Divine Milieu* (New York: Harper Torchbooks, 1965), 74.

serves as the fulfillment, the denouement, of life. It uses the fruits of our labor that was inspired and inanimate by God to transport us beyond our limitations and sinfulness into eternal communion with God. Ministry that is catholic enables all people to participate in the metamorphosis of creation through the cross of Christ into the reign of God.[16]

---

[16] Ibid., 104. See also, Donald C. Maldari, SJ, "The Evolution of the Messianic Age: The Metamorphosis from Competitive Selfishness to Selfless, Altruistic, Cooperative Love," *Louvain Studies* 36 (2012): 372–96.

Chapter 1

The Immanent and Transcendent Aspects of the Church

"Where are you coming you from, and where are you going?" Socrates (c. 470–399 BCE) hauntingly asks Phaedrus in the first line of Plato's *Dialog* of the same name. Socrates's question isn't just about what Phaedrus had been doing just before their chance meeting in Athens and what he was planning on doing immediately afterward. Socrates's question challenges Phaedrus—and all of us—to put our lives in a larger context. He challenges us to consider where we are now in light of our past and hoped-for future. This challenge can be very disruptive, especially when we are under the impression that we've got a good handle on everything. I recall an experience I had when I was about seven or eight years old. I took a walk around the neighborhood where we lived with my parents and some friends. I remember being mildly upset to learn that the neighborhood was much bigger than I had thought. I had a mini–Copernican revolution experience. Not only was our house not the center of the universe, but it wasn't even the center of the neighborhood! Who knew? Since then I've learned that not only is the universe far vaster than I can ever imagine, but it's also continually changing.

Modern science proved the ancient Greek philosopher Heraclitus (c. 535–475 BCE) right when he proposed that everything in the universe is changing. Curiously, that same

17

Heraclitus proposed that the source of all things and the principle that keeps it all together is the Logos—the Word—the same term that Christians use to name the Son, through whom the Father creates all things. The Logos, the Word, the Son, who is the revelation of the Father, is the principle of stability in creation (see Mal 3:6; Heb 13:8). Heraclitus's vision finds an echo in the prayer that accompanies the beginning of the Easter Vigil as the Paschal candle is inscribed with the first and last letters of the Greek alphabet:

> Christ yesterday and today,
> the beginning and the end,
> Alpha and Omega,
> all time belongs to him,
> and all ages;
> to him be glory and power,
> through every age and forever. Amen.

Copernican revolutions often don't sit well with Christians. Galileo found that out the hard way as he spent the last nine years of his life under house arrest for disagreeing with church authorities about the movement of the sun. Despite the fears of new ideas by church authorities in the seventeenth century, Copernicus's and Galileo's theories, which were pretty much on target, did not threaten the Christian faith. In fact, knowing more about how creation works helps us to know more about its Creator. Moreover, knowing more about how creation works helps us to know more about our role in it. We are creatures who actively contribute to and participate in the changing universe of which Heraclitus spoke. The authors of the Book of Genesis sensed that responsibility when they describe God giving humanity the charge to fill the earth, subdue it, and have dominion over it (Gen 1:28).

This little meditation on context and change is meant as an invitation to situate human life and activity into its larger context. Where has human life come from? Are there patterns in our evolutionary history that give hints about where we might be going? Is there actually a destination? Are there things that people can do to help us get to our destination? Alternately, are there activities in which people can engage that do serious damage to the human journey, maybe even stop us in our tracks? Amid all the flux and change, is there any stability at all? Questions such as these arose in the mind and soul of Pierre Teilhard de Chardin as he contemplated the evidence of human evolution from both an immanent and transcendent perspective. The *Human Phenomenon*,[1] one of his greatest works, traces the development of humanity largely from the immanent perspective, beginning with what he calls the "stuff"[2] of the universe down to our day. Many of his other works, most notably *The Divine Milieu*,[3] contemplate the evidence largely from the transcendent perspective.

Like Teilhard we will look at the questions of our origins from both their immanent and transcendent dimensions. Looking at the immanent dimension of our reality, we'll situate ourselves in the vast context of the evolution of the universe. Where have we come from, in the sense of our physical antecedents? How has our species, Homo sapiens, come to be what it is? What does this history tell us about our role in the evolving universe? Looking at the transcendent dimension of reality, we'll situate ourselves in the vast context of salvation history. Where have we come from, in the sense of our divine antecedents? Why has humanity come to be what it is? Where are we going, in the sense of our divine predestination? What does the history of salvation tell us about our role in the divine

---

[1] Pierre Teilhard de Chardin, *The Human Phenomenon*, trans. Sarah Appleton-Weber (Portland, OR: Sussex Academic Press, 1999). Originally published as *Le phénomène humain* (Paris: Éditions du Seuil, 1955).

[2] *L'étoffe* in French. This word could also be translated into English as "cloth, fabric, or tissue." In the 1999 English edition of *The Human Phenomenon*, Sarah Appleton-Weber translates it as "stuff."

[3] Pierre Teilhard de Chardin, *The Divine Milieu* (New York: Harper, 1960). Originally published as *Le Milieu Divin* (Paris: Éditions du Seuil, 1957).

plan to bring creation to fulfillment? The proposed answers may be unsettling. But I hope they expand our horizons so as to help us participate more fully and effectively in God's plan of salvation.

The Challenge of Talking about the Church

Back in 381 CE the second ecumenical council met in the imperial capital of Constantinople. The Emperor Theodosius I called the council together mainly to deal with disputes among Christians concerning the Holy Spirit. The assembled bishops eventually hammered out a document based upon a baptismal statement of faith extant at the time. That document is now known as the Nicene Creed. God only knows why people call this new creed by the name of one produced fifty-six years earlier in Nicaea; it was not a reworking of the old creed but a brand-new one. Whatever the reason, the new Creed contained an elaborate section on the Holy Spirit that was lacking in the creed by the Council of Nicaea. It expressed the Christian belief that the Holy Spirit is divine, personal, and a full member of the Holy Trinity along with the Father and the Son. It described the Holy Spirit as proceeding from the Father and as the person who inspires the prophets, through whom he speaks. The creed elaborates the work of the Holy Spirit by including what Christians believe about the church, including what they acknowledge about baptism and the forgiveness of sins, and what we look forward to in the resurrection of the dead and the life in the age to come.

A careful reading of the original Greek text and its Latin translation of the creed of the Council of Constantinople shows that it has three, not four parts: one on the Father, one on the Son, one on the Holy Spirit. The council beautifully situates all existence within the Holy Trinity. The section about the church is really a subsection of the section on the Spirit. The council fathers believed that the church flows from the Spirit.

The transcendent insight of the fathers of the Council of Constantinople finds a parallel in the immanent theories of how the universe works proposed by the natural sciences. What the fathers called the church is the product of the interaction of matter and energy as described by the laws of thermodynamics. That may appear mindboggling—enticingly so! With the eyes of reason and the eyes of faith we can trace the development of what we call the church right back to the Big Bang! Even Saint Thomas Aquinas thought that the church can trace its history as far back as Abel in the Book of Genesis.[4]

Before going back 13.7 billion years, let's take a look at the ever-evolving moving target that we call the church in the twenty-first century. People assume that they know what they're talking about when they use the word *church,* but in fact it means very different things to different people. I have encountered this semantic bedlam in the ecclesiology courses that I have taught over the years. The meanings of *church* for students include a building; a local, national, or international organization; the hierarchy of clergy, bishops, and pope; some vague entity known as the Vatican; a sovereign country; a corporation; and some nondescript religious organization. All of them, to some degree, are right. In his landmark book, first published in 1974, *Models of the Church,*[5] Avery Dulles put some order into this ecclesiastical din by identifying first five and then, in the late 1970s, six ways of imaging and thinking about what the church is. He called these ways "models." Those models are institution, mystical communion, sacrament, herald, servant, and community of disciples. He understands

---

[4] Thomas Aquinas, *The Aquinas Catechism: A Simple Explanation of the Catholic Faith by the Church's Greatest Theologian* (Manchester, NH: Sophia Institute Press, 2000), 81, art. IX; *In symbolum Apostolorum, Opusculum VII* (Parma edn.), vol. xvi, pp. 135–51, at art. IX, p. 148. "Some have said that the Church will exist only up to a certain time. But this is false, for the Church began to exist in the time of Abel and will endure up to the end of the world."

[5] Avery Dulles, *Models of the Church* (Garden City, NY: Doubleday, 1987).

these models as complementary, and points out that none of them is completely accurate. Christians have to choose one of them, though not necessarily forever, as their paradigm. This paradigm serves to guide the church's self-consciousness and organization. The only model he rejects as a candidate for a paradigm is that of institution. He recognizes that the church has to organize itself, but—and this is very important—its primary identity is not to be an institution. The institutional aspect of the church must be at the service of whatever paradigm people choose. If, for example, Christians decide to think of the church primarily as the people of God, which falls into his mystical communion model and was the choice of the Second Vatican Council, then whatever organizational, institutional structure it develops must effectively serve that paradigm. The institution must not take on a life of its own. It's there to help Christians live the model they choose as the primary one for their self-identity as church, not the other way around. This will be essential to keep in mind when we discuss the hierarchical structure of the church in Chapter 4. Whatever model Christians choose—and there's no reason why we have to stick to the same one if a changing environment suggests that a different one would be preferable—the church has to organize its members in such a way that all members have the opportunity to express and use their gifts and talents for the good of the whole. This requirement flows right out of a consideration of the data that explain the church's identity drawn from the immanent and transcendent dimensions of reality. So, let's take a look.

Where Have We Come from and Where Are We Going? The Immanent Dimension through Physics

Let's imagine that we have use of the DeLorean automobile made famous by the 1985 film *Back to the Future*. We travel through time back to the Big Bang without interfering with the events of the past—in reality an impossible task, but since this is our imagination we can do whatever we want.

First of all, what is the Big Bang? It's a theory first proposed in 1927 by the Belgian Catholic priest Georges Lemaître (though the term itself came later). Lemaître studied the interplay between energy and matter in the universe, which is expanding. He proposed that this expanding universe could be traced back to a single moment that was an explosion of pure energy. From the safety of our DeLorean we are witnessing the answer to Socrates's question in a bigger way than he had imagined: where we came from 13.7 billion years ago. Immediately after the greatest cosmic flash of all time, energy began being turned into matter. Scientists define energy as the capacity to work, in other words, the "stuff," to use Teilhard's expression, that makes it possible for things to happen. One of the measures of energy is calories—something anyone who eats is familiar with. The energy we get from eating food is what makes it possible to be alive and do stuff. If we don't do stuff but keep eating, we store that energy as fat, usually in unflattering places on our bodies.

Physicists tell us that the events in the first second after the Big Bang were, well, astronomical. Suffice it to say for our purposes that a pattern developed almost instantly, one which we call the laws of thermodynamics. As we observe what is going on from our DeLorean, we see that energy and matter are interchangeable forms of the same stuff that constitutes the universe. That stuff can take the form of energy or the form of matter. Regardless of what form it takes, the amount of stuff remains the same. This is, in a simple, bare-bones way, the first law of thermodynamics (conservation of energy and matter). In a more sophisticated way we can say that neither energy nor matter can be created or destroyed. A corollary of this statement is that the amount of stuff in the universe is finite.

As we continue to gaze at the birth of the universe from the comfort of our DeLorean, we notice a pattern of how energy and matter interact and change forms from one to another. We witness the distribution of energy and its effect on matter. Starting right from the Big Bang, energy began to spread throughout the universe. If we were to personalize energy in our imagination—something that scientists without much imagination cringe at—we could think of energy as having the desire to be distributed evenly everywhere. Billions of years later, when we return to the twenty-first century, we'll be able to see energy's "desire" in action on a broiling summer day in a house on earth when one room is air conditioned and the adjacent one is not. Physicists call this an *energy gradient* and the two rooms they'd refer to as *systems*. When you open the door between the two rooms (now two open systems) the heat from the room that is not air conditioned rushes into the one that is air conditioned. That's because all the little air molecules in the hot room have a lot more energy than the ones in the cool room. They bounce around a lot, and they bounce right into the cold room, heating it up. Nature is egalitarian. It doesn't like energy gradients, that is, it doesn't want some places to have more energy (in this case be hot) and others to have less energy (here, be cold). It wants everything to be evenly distributed. In the end, if we leave the door between the two rooms open long enough, the temperature in them will be the same. There will be more energy in the air-conditioned room than there was before and less energy in the room that is not air conditioned. On a more global level, nature's pursuit of equality is the cause of major wind storms such as hurricanes and tornadoes. These storms may be a bit of an exaggeration of nature's magnanimity when they cause a lot of destruction, but they are essential for the earth's ecosystem. They serve to redistribute energy throughout the planet to make most of it habitable by us.

The distribution of energy from higher concentrations to lower ones is what physicists call the second law of thermodynamics. If we return to the first few seconds after the Big Bang, we'll see it at work. Energy was unevenly distributed in the universe. This means that there are energy gradients in the universe just as there are between an air-conditioned room and a hot room in the summer. Mother Nature does not like energy gradients. Energy, therefore, is constantly being redistributed throughout the universe so that everything gets its fair share, as it were. As energy is redistributed it becomes matter—remember the first law of thermodynamics. In fact, energy cleverly organizes matter with the result that matter helps to distribute energy. How? Energy propels molecules that move around a lot until those molecules find compatible molecules to which they join. Sometimes the union is temporary but sometimes it's long lasting. The long-lasting unions form those systems to which I referred above. As more and different energized molecules join together they form increasingly complex systems. These more complex systems require more energy to sustain themselves. That means, they work.

Over the past 13.7 billion years energy has been very busy moving among open systems, that is, systems that are able to receive or give away energy. They move from systems with more energy—a higher energy gradient—to those with less energy—a lower energy gradient. As they do so two phenomena occur. One is that the system that receives energy becomes more complex. Systems themselves don't usually have much personality, but if we anthropomorphize the transfer of energy we might say that matter becomes more complex in order to dissipate energy ever more efficiently. The more energy, the more sophisticated the system, the better it spreads energy around, fulfilling energy's altruistic nature, as it were. Okay, for any purists out there: nothing in science has an intentional purpose and, no, energy is not of itself altruistic.

As systems become more and more sophisticated, we tend to say that they are alive. The line between animate and inanimate is so difficult to draw that it may not actually exist. Atoms and molecules in objects such as rocks, which we call inanimate, all move. They're just not as sophisticated a system as the atoms and molecules in plants and animals. Nick Lane, who teaches evolutionary biochemistry at University College London, writes: "Plainly there is a continuum between non-living and living, and it is pointless to try to draw a line across it."[6] The application of Occam's Razor, the philosophical principle that the most simple complete explanation for something is the best, appears to prompt Lane to look with suspicion on NASA's working definition of life: "a self-sustaining chemical system capable of Darwinian evolution."[7] We humans exist in a remarkable if humbling continuum with the rest of the universe. The exact same essential physical patterns characterize the development of all systems in the universe, including us.

The second phenomenon that occurs thanks to the second law of thermodynamics is that systems that lose energy become less complex. Work dissipates energy. It redistributes it. The redistribution of energy means that energy gradients are diminished and, in the very long run, destroyed. Systems with more energy distribute that energy to systems with less energy, thus making Mother Nature very happy. On the other hand, as energy is redistributed and energy gradients leveled out, there is more and more matter and less and less energy. Remember, energy and matter are just two forms of the same stuff, and that the amount of that stuff in the universe is finite. The ever-more-successful distribution of energy means there is less energy around to organize matter. This is known as entropy. The increase in entropy means a decrease in order and organization.

Life, including humanity, is actually increasingly more successful products of the evolutionary process that distributes energy throughout the universe in increasingly more efficient ways. We are, in this sense, increasingly perfecting and advancing our own demise. Human work—human activity—contributes to moving the universe toward its denouement. Complex systems of matter that distribute energy leave systems in their wake with

---

[6] Nick Lane, *The Vital Question: Energy, Evolution, and the Origins of Complex Life* (New York: W. W. Norton, 2016), 55. See also Arto Annila and Erkki Annila, "Why Did Life Emerge?" *International Journal of Astrobiology* 7 (2008): 293–300; Arthur Peacocke, "Thermodynamics and Life," *Zygon* 19 (1984): 395–432.

[7] Lane, *The Vital Question: Energy, Evolution, and the Origins of Complex Life*, 55.

increasingly less energy to organize them. In the really, really long run this means that the universe is winding down at an increasing rate thanks to the increasing efficiency of systems to distribute energy. The current long-term meteorological projection is for an extremely cold universe. In the "Big End" all energy shall have been equally distributed, all energy shall become matter, and with no energy there is nothing with which to work and produce heat. The universe will sink to 0 on the Kelvin scale, or −273.15 on the Celsius scale or −459.67 on the Fahrenheit scale. The universe, and any surviving humans, will "die."

It is important to note here that from the perspective of physics *all* human work participates in and contributes to the process of equally distributing energy throughout the universe. The human activity that causes climate change on our little planet, for example, is, from the standpoint of physics, a major contribution to the more equitable distribution of energy. That it may well lead to the demise of our species is, from the perspective of physics, the unfortunate extinction of a really successful energy-distributing system. We're doing our bit to cool off the universe.[8]

Where Have We Come from and Where Are We Going? The Immanent Dimension through Biocultural Evolution

Physicists predict that the universe still has a couple of billion good years ahead of it, so it's worth our while to keep studying what role we humans play before universal retirement kicks in. People, Homo sapiens, are the result of billions of years of evolution. We are relatively young on the global scene. We are approximately a mere 2.8 million years old on a planet that is approximately 4.5 billion years old. We've had a rocky road. About seventy-four-thousand years ago we nearly became extinct due to climate change; the whole species may have had

---

[8] See Eric D. Schneider and Dorion Sagan, *Into the Cool* (Chicago: University of Chicago Press, 2005).

only about ten thousand adults. Other species very similar to us did become extinct: about seventy thousand years ago Homo erectus disappeared, about twenty-eight thousand years ago Neanderthals became extinct, and about seventeen thousand years ago Homo floresiensis disappeared. We alone survived. What is the secret of our success?

Scientists identify at least two reasons why species survive. One is *natural selection,* by which species as a whole have enough members that can adapt to changing environmental conditions such as weather, food supplies, predators, and so on. Another is genetic mutations that provide new characteristics in individual members of species. These new characteristics may prove very helpful in adapting better to the environment or multiple environments.

In fact, nowadays natural selection and genetic mutations are not the main ways we humans evolve. Human culture, activity that we consciously devise in order to promote our development, plays an essential part in our evolution.[9] We organize and program what we do in relation to what we want to achieve. In other words, we consciously or unconsciously have some notion of what success looks like, and we work to achieve it. We engage in horticulture and agriculture with some idea of what a successful crop will be. We do the same in "*human*culture." We grow ourselves. We could say that is what *religio* was before the Enlightenment. People organized their lives to fulfill their duty to arrive at an eternal goal.

We humans are so intellectually bright that humanculture is wildly successful. Physically we are nothing to write home about. We are no match in evolution to faster and more powerful species. Add brains and conscience to the mix, however, and we're dynamite. Not only do we survive, but we multiply at alarming rates! We are able to manipulate our environment in such a way as to direct the trajectory of our planet's evolu-

---

[9] See Philip Hefner, "The Spiritual Task of Religion in Culture: An Evolutionary Perspective," *Zygon* 33 (1998): 535–44.

tion, for better or for worse. Many species can manipulate their environment to increase their chances of survival: birds build nests, beavers build dams, ants build underground tunnels. But no other species manipulates the environment as well as we do: skyscrapers, plumbing, electricity, heating, and so forth. These are all products of our great capacity to reason and to understand the immanent dimension of reality. Once we have built habitats that favor our physical survival, we go on to produce symbols, that is, works of art. These are the products of our great capacity to see beyond the immanent dimension of reality to the transcendent. They, too, play an essential role in human survival. Art—whether visual, audio, ritual, theater, or another expression—communicates insights into the human condition. It influences how people approach our future. Culture plays such a large role in human evolution that anthropologists speak of biocultural evolution.[10]

We humans have also developed a trait we call *conscience*. We cannot know if any other species have developed the same trait, but we do know that we have. Conscience is our capacity to distinguish good from bad not only in the immanent dimension of reality—which in one form or another everything can—but also in the transcendent dimension. It provides us with the moral responsibility to promote the evolution of the universe toward its ultimate fulfillment. Strictly speaking, only humans can be benevolent or malicious. Accusing other species of being malicious, as when a dog misbehaves in the house, is projection of the human capacity for evil onto the poor canine, who really doesn't have that capacity. All activities of all beings except humans please God. Only humans are capable of sin. Conscience has developed through natural selection and

---

[10] See, for example, Mark V. Flinn and Richard D. Alexander, "Culture Theory: The Developing Synthesis from Biology," *Human Ecology* 10 (1982): 383–400; Philip Hefner, "The Spiritual Task of Religion in Culture: An Evolutionary Perspective," *Zygon* 33 (1998): 535–44; Martin A. Nowak, "Five Rules for the Evolution of Cooperation," *Science* 314 (2006): 1560–63.

biocultural evolution. Since it has survived as a human trait, it must serve some purpose in promoting human survival. It helps us to develop into the fullness of humanity, what theology calls *saints*.

Nature has bequeathed on humanity instincts for both cooperative and competitive behaviors. These instincts, which we share with other eusocial species such as ants and bees, help us to develop an extraordinary human culture. Thanks to geographical distribution human culture consists of a myriad of forms. They are manifest in scientific research, the development of technology, artistic expression, and so on. We develop and engage in these activities to promote our survival. This much reason alone can tell us. Faith tells us that what survival ultimately looks like transcends our wildest imaginations.

Human work is a practical expression of human culture. It not only draws upon our evolutionary heritage, but it also shapes our evolutionary future. An essential element in biocultural evolution, of which human work is a part, has been the development of patterns of cooperation and competition in our species. Scientists now recognize that cooperation plays an essential role in all of evolution. We see it in the formation of eukaryotic cells with symbiotic organelles. These cells have DNA in the form of chromosomes inside a nucleus and organized structures. These cells are themselves composed of molecules that have bonded as a result of energy and serve to degrade energy. The eukaryotic cells are the next stage of the evolutionary process that promotes increasingly efficient ways of degrading energy. Joan Strassmann et al. observe: "Major transitions in the hierarchy of life have often involved cooperation among lower-level units to the point where they evolve into higher-level organisms." They propose: "Cooperation has been central to humanity's spectacular success and will be central to our short- and long-term fates."[11]

---

[11] Joan E. Strassmann, David C. Queller, John C. Avise, and Francisco J. Ayala, "In the Light of Evolution V: Cooperation and Conflict," *PNAS* 108 (2011): 10787.

Altruism and Selfishness

There is no shortage of studies of the roles of cooperation and of competition in evolution. These studies are being done in the areas of the natural as well as social sciences, and even extend to mathematics. Evolution has bequeathed us with an instinct for self-preservation on the individual and communal level. That instinct takes a number of different forms, all inherited from our evolutionary ancestors. The whole point of whatever we do is to survive. All systems compete to get as much energy as possible in an environment with only a limited amount of energy. For example, trees grow as quickly and as tall as possible in order to get as much sun as possible. Or plants, in a plant-like resignation that they simply are not going to grow into the plant equivalent of NBA stars, adapt to their short stature and require less light to grow in the forest. They nevertheless establish their own niche in the forest and compete with other short plants for nutrients. The same principle of competition operates in successful species of animals, including human beings. We are often proud of our competitive nature, which encourages us to strive for success in the struggle for survival.

Competition is not the only strategy for success in survival. Evolution also demonstrates the value of cooperation, even to the point of self-sacrificing altruism. This occurs on all levels of system complexity. We see it at the molecular level as some primordial RNA probably replicated itself not simply by copying itself but developed cooperative self-assembly cycles after being fragmented. This process gave these molecules an advantage over those RNA molecules that selfishly simply replicated themselves.[12] On the level of individual organisms we see cooperation and altruism at work in the humble slime molds, *Dictyostelium discoideum*, affectionately known as Dicty. Dicty is an amoeba that sends signals to other individuals of its species when food or moisture is insufficient to sustain

---

[12] James Attwater and Philipp Holliger, "Origins of Life: The Co-operative Gene," *Nature* 491 (November 2012): 48–49.

its life. Other individuals respond to form a large gathering, sometimes reaching 100,000. This gathering acts as one to promote locomotion of which one individual cell would be incapable. The group forms a base and stalk to promote movement and communication; the cells in these areas of the group lose their ability to reproduce, offering up their future for the good of the whole, while other cells become spores.[13] Groups within a species and whole species engage in this behavior. Biologist David Sloan Wilson reflects on the evolutionary process by which humans have been so successful: "As soon as egalitarianism became sufficiently established, genetic evolution started to reshape our minds and bodies to function as team players rather than competing against members of our own groups."[14] He notes that humans have developed methods of communication that no other species has: eyes with small irises so others can see what we are looking at, pointing that is understood as a direction, laughter and smiling, and, of course, complex speech. At the same time, there are individuals who promote their own survival, even at the expense of others in the group. Nevertheless, species where cooperative behavior prevails are the most successful in the competition for survival: ants and bees are among the most cooperative and numerous species on earth. Finally, ecosystems develop cooperative characteristics as envisioned, for example, by Thomas Berry in an emerging "ecozoic age."[15] The altruistic behavior of most of this cooperation, however, is ultimately selfish; it aims at survival by securing enough energy through cooperative

---

[13] David Sloan Wilson, *Evolution for Everyone* (New York: Bantam-Dell, 2007), 129–32. See also Kenneth R. Miller, *Finding Darwin's God* (New York: HarperCollins, 1999), 247–48; Francis S. Collins, *The Language of God* (New York: Free Press, 2006), 28.

[14] Wilson, *Evolution for Everyone,* 165.

[15] Thomas Berry, "The Emerging Ecozoic Period," *Cooperation: Beyond the Age of Competition*, ed. Allan Combs (Amsterdam: Gordon and Breach Science Publishers, 1992), 181–84.

competition.[16] Patterns of human behavior are currently being studied in a new area called game theory. Computers are programmed to simulate strategies that people would develop in a variety of circumstances when they are faced with the dilemma of cooperating with others or not.[17] It gets pretty complicated. Ultimately, however, the most successful strategies are those that optimize the paybacks for whatever we do, whether it be to cooperate or to betray other people.

In the short run the best strategy is actually to be individualistic and selfish. People are naturally selfish: it is an instinct that we have inherited through evolution. We've inherited it and

---

[16] See Martin A. Nowak and Natalia L. Kamarova, "The Evolution of Altruism: From Game Theory to Human Language," *Spiritual Information: 100 Perspectives on Science and Religion: Essays in Honor of Sir John Templeton's 90th Birthday,* ed. Charles L. Harper, Jr. (Philadelphia: Templeton Foundation Press, 2005), 308–14; Robert Axelrod, *The Evolution of Cooperation* (New York: Basic Books, 1984); Martin A. Nowak with Roger Highfield, *SuperCooperators: Altruism, Evolution, and Why We Need Each Other to Succeed* (New York: Free Press, 2011); Björn Vollan and Elinor Ostrom, "Cooperation and the Commons," *Science* 330 (2010): 923–24.

[17] See Claudia Canegallo et al., "Competition Versus Cooperation: Some Experimental Evidence," *The Journal of Socio-Economics* 37 (2008): 18–30; Carsten K. W. De Dreu and Christopher McCusker, "Gain-Loss Frames and Cooperation in Two-Person Social Dilemmas: A Transformational Analysis," *Journal of Personality and Social Psychology* 72 (1997): 1093–106; David G. Rand and Martin A. Nowak, "Human Cooperation," *Trends in Cognitive Sciences* 17 (2013): 413–25; David G. Rand et al., "Religious Motivations for Cooperation: An Experimental Investigation Using Explicit Primes," *Religion, Brain and Behavior* 4 (2014): 31–48; Martin A. Nowak et al., eds., *Evolution, Games, and God: The Principle of Cooperation* (Cambridge: Harvard University Press, 2013); Martin A. Nowak, *Evolutionary Dynamics* (Cambridge: Belknap Press, 2006); Martin A. Nowak, "Why We Help," *Scientific American* 307 (2012): 34–39; Martin A. Nowak, "The Evolution of Eusociality," *Nature* 466 (2010): 1057–62; David G. Rand et al., "Positive Interactions Promote Public Cooperation," *Science* 425 (2009): 1272–75.

practice it because there is some advantage to it in natural selection. But in the long run people recognize that altruism and the cooperation it leads to also pay off. Scientists demonstrate the cyclical nature of altruism/cooperation and selfishness/competition. People will join together into cooperative groups that serve to promote success to a degree and in ways that they would not attain if they worked only as independent individuals. The groups are characterized by altruistic, even self-sacrificing behavior to promote the good of the group. Indeed, the group has a kind of personal identity and spirit, such as teams, tribes, neighborhoods, ethnic groups, or nations. Competition with other groups for the same resources—ultimately, access to energy that literally keeps us together—is a strong motivation for altruism and cooperation within a group. When the external threat of competition for resources diminishes, however, there is less incentive for altruism and cooperation. Individual members of the group cheat. Just think of graft and corruption in large businesses, government, sports teams, and so on. Eventually other members of the group realize that they are being duped. More members of the group give up on altruism and grab whatever they can. In the meantime, other people form new cooperative groups to compete with this old one, and as the old group disintegrates the new ones develop and flourish.

Studying the immanent dimension of reality from the perspective of reason alone provides no reason to think that this cycle of increased and decreased cooperation is anything but vicious. It is the pattern for survival that has developed through natural selection. E. O. Wilson, who is a specialist in social insects such as bees and ants, holds that the same social instinct is operative in humans:

> The pathway to eusociality was chartered by a contest between selection based on the relative success of individuals within groups versus relative success among groups. The strategies of this game were written as a complicated mix of closely calibrated altruism,

cooperation, competition, domination, reciprocity, de-
fection, and deceit.[18]

Wilson concludes that the cycle of altruistic and selfish behavior springs from the very essence of human nature. We are all,
he writes, "part saint and part sinner." There is absolutely no
way out that would lead to universal and eternal altruism and
cooperation.[19]

Martin Nowak, a professor of biology and mathematics and
director of the Program for Evolutionary Dynamics at Harvard
University, understands the cycle of altruism/cooperation and
selfishness/competition in the same way as Wilson. Unlike Wilson, however, he also peers into the transcendent dimension of
reality, where he perceives hope. The last chapter of his book
SuperCooperators is a meditation on Gustav Mahler's *The
Song of the Earth*. Nowak reports what he perceives through
the medium of music:

> But in the darkness of the symphony a chink of brilliant
> optimism can be glimpsed, along with a sense of surprise,
> which Mahler signals with a final change into the key of
> C major. At the moment that Mahler is reconciled with
> his own mortality, he understands how extinction will be
> followed by a new spring. This carries a deep resonance
> for me and my work.[20]

His hope echoes that of Teilhard, who, after tracing human
evolution through the universe's history, concludes that without "a higher pole of attraction and consistency," without the
influence of an "Omega Center," "life can neither continue to
function or to progress." Teilhard perceives the personal energy
of Christ, who is the Holy Spirit, working through human
culture to cooperate with God in bringing creation beyond

---

[18] E. O. Wilson, *The Social Conquest of Earth* (New York: Liveright
Publishing/W. W. Norton, 2012), 17.

[19] Ibid., 289.

[20] Nowak and Highfield, *SuperCooperators*, 280.

its limitations.[21] Through faith Teilhard and Nowak, both scientists, have reason to hope that the vicious cycle of altruism and selfishness can be broken. Ministry is work that builds that culture leading to human transcendence. Our ministry is co-creative work with the Creator.

Overcoming the Altruism-Selfishness Dilemma

As we have seen, under the influence of energy matter becomes increasingly complex as a means of degrading energy, that is, as a means of distributing it equally throughout the universe. As energy gradients are leveled, less energy is available to organize matter, resulting in entropy, that is, less organization. The result, as we have seen, is that the current long-term prognosis for the universe is what is popularly called death. Taking the macro view of the development of the universe, the Big Bang, culminates in the Big Whimper, to paraphrase T. S. Eliot. This at-first-sight bleak future raises fundamental questions: Why bother? Is existence much ado about nothing? The micro view of the value of human work raises the same fundamental questions. We are born, engage in some forms of education, work, most people reproduce, and then we die. Why? Is Shakespeare's pessimism justified when he writes:

> All the world's a stage,
> And all the men and women merely players;
> They have their exits and their entrances;
> And one man in his time plays many parts,
> His acts being seven ages....
> Last scene of all,
> That ends this strange eventful history,
> Is second childishness and mere oblivion;

---

[21] Teilhard de Chardin, *The Human Phenomenon*, 209–23; *Le Phénomène Humain*, 324–44. See also Ilia Delio, *Christ in Evolution* (Maryknoll, NY: Orbis Books, 2008), 66–82.

> Sans teeth, sans eyes, sans taste, sans everything.
> —*As You Like It*, Act II, Scene VII

The increased consciousness/conscience of matter, which "enfolds of itself," to use Teilhard's terminology, suggests otherwise.

Consciousness is awareness of our environment. With increased consciousness comes increased awareness. As far as we know from observation, all of what we call animals are conscious and therefore aware of their environment. Some appear to be more conscious than others.[22] Regardless of the degree of consciousness of other beings are earth, we humans have developed an extraordinary capacity for consciousness. We even call ourselves Homo sapiens (wise human). Conscious and conscience have the same etymological root in Latin, *conscire*, meaning "to be aware, to know with." The increased awareness that Teilhard attributes to us allows us to see that matter becomes more complex and enfolded. We become increasingly aware of both how our environment works (the immanent dimension of reality) and why it works (the transcendent dimension of reality). Knowledge of the why, of the meaning of reality, leads us to formulate our ultimate goal. We, the players on Shakespeare's stage, write the play in light of our perceived ultimate goal. We act, we work, in such a way as to promote that goal. Or we ought to!

Where Have We Come from and Where Are We Going? The Transcendent Dimension

Our consideration of our extremely distant origins back to the Big Bang used reason alone. Scientists study hard data about the state of our universe and reason backward to the universe's likely beginning. A reasonable person can discuss, challenge,

---

[22] See Carl Safina, *Beyond Words* (New York: Picador, 2015).

revise, and expand these scientific interpretations using reason alone. Pure Enlightenment thinking claims that this is *all* that we can know. As we saw in the Introduction, Enlightenment thinkers hold that the only way to know anything is through reason; they deny that faith can teach us anything about reality.

The limitation of knowledge to reason alone is not satisfactory for most people. We cannot use popularity to judge the validity of a theory, but it does invite us to ask questions. Reason alone consigns human emotions to chemical, endocrinological changes that are the result of natural selection in Darwinian evolution. They may, indeed, be such, but are they nothing more? Is love nothing but a physical phenomenon? Is inspiration really only an inherited characteristic that has some use in survival? Is art nothing but a form of communication among humans with no outside source? As mentioned earlier, English poet Samuel Taylor Coleridge, in the wake of Enlightenment reasoning, pled for "that willing suspension of disbelief for the moment, which constitutes poetic faith."[23] It is the contention of Christianity and a large number of other cultures that faith opens our eyes to the other dimension of reality: the transcendent.

The authors of the Bible looked upon the immanent dimension of reality through the eyes of faith and saw the transcendent. That Homo sapiens has evolved from the Big Bang as an outstanding open system that degrades energy does not contradict the stories in the Book of Genesis that describe the creation of Adam and Eve. Unfortunately, an apparent contradiction has been a cause of polemic and anxiety for some and the cause of the rejection of Judeo-Christian faith for others. The controversy really is, however, much ado about nothing.

Ever since the nineteenth century scripture scholars have developed a number of literary tools, called criticisms, to interpret the Bible. Two of those criticisms are of particular use to us here to understand the insights of the creation stories. The first is called *form criticism*. This tool tries to identify the

---

[23] *Biographia Literaria* (London: Rest Fenner, 1817).

literary form or genre of texts. Ignorance of literary forms can result in awkward situations. Imagine a person's surprise when he or she learns that George Orwell's book *1984* is not a work of history but of fiction! History and fiction are two legitimate literary forms, both of which try to express an author's insight. People sometimes have difficulty in seeing how fiction can express truth. By definition, fiction is at best a white lie; the facts are either all made up or so freely manipulated as to be untrustworthy for recounting what historically happened. People don't write fiction, however, to recount what happened. They tell us upfront that their story is fiction and may or may not contain historical facts. Good literary fiction is not an escape *from* reality but insight *into* reality. Authors stimulate our imaginations through Coleridge's "willing suspension of disbelief" in order to propose transcendent truth through the immanent medium of a story.

When using form criticism, it is also useful to identify the historical context in which a piece of literature was written. Authors don't write in historical vacuums. They are products of their environments, and they write for real people whom they know. They use images that are meaningful to those real people. Again, Orwell's novel *1984* provides a good illustration of the importance of identifying not only the literary form but also the historical context. Orwell wrote his novel in 1948; he just reversed the last two digits of the year in the novel's title. The year 1948 was in an early period of the Cold War. Orwell projected the logical conclusion of the totalitarian Eastern European governments, in particular the Soviet Union, into what the world would look like thirty-six years later. Thirty-six years was far enough away for people to have a sense of hope that change was possible, but it was close enough to scare people into action. And that is exactly what Orwell wanted to do.

Another tool we'll need to use in order to understand what the Genesis creation stories are trying to say is *source criticism*. Alas, we have no idea who the author of the Book of Genesis was. Scripture scholars have spent a lot of time and effort trying to work that out. They tell us that because so many people contributed to the text over a very long period of time—we're talking centuries—that it is more accurate to speak of a "source" rather than an "author." German scholars in the nineteenth century studied the different writing styles, vocabulary, and themes of the first five books of the Old Testament and proposed they were composed by four different sources. (I use the same technique when I notice different styles of writing in student essays and wonder if there might be more than one author.) Those German scripture scholars named the sources after the first letter of their German names. This became J (Yahwist), E (Elohist), P (Priestly), and D (Deuteronomist). An editor later put the texts of all these sources together in a way that made sense, at least to the editor.

Using form criticism we identify the literary genre of the first few chapters of the Book of Genesis as etiological myth. When scripture scholars identify a passage as myth, they do not mean something that is not true, in the sense that many people commonly use the word. A myth for scripture scholars is a fictional story that intends to communicate insights into reality. An etiological myth expresses insights into the character of something that we know by telling a fictional story of its origins. In Oceania, where I now live, there are many myths about the origin of a plant commonly called kava. Kava is made into a drink that has tremendous ritual significance and power in the cultures of the Pacific islands. It is often called the drink of the gods that the gods gave to people. This is because it has the effect of heightening people's awareness, of bringing people together, and of reconciling people who need reconciling. The various myths of its origins tell stories about why kava has this effect. The etiological myths of creation in Genesis do not intend to describe how but why God creates the universe. They describe what the authors think is the character of the creation.

The first two chapters of Genesis present their reader with a puzzle if one does not use literary criticism; they tell the story of creation twice. In the first story God creates everything in six days and rests on the seventh. We get the impression that the story is finished, and we're ready to move on to see how the story unfolds. But as we read chapter 2 God starts creating all over again. This time there's already a Garden of Eden—we don't know where this came from—but no animals. God starts off by creating Adam out of a clay figure, then moves on to animals, and finally, when Adam complains he's lonely, God creates Eve.

Putting on our detective hats we look at the evidence and try to figure out what is going on with these two stories. Using form criticism we identify the two stories as etiological myths; using source criticism we suspect that the first story was by the P (Priestly) source and the second by the J (Yahwist) source. The P source took form probably in the sixth century BCE and the J source probably in the ninth century BCE. P put his story first because he got there last.

Having identified the literary form of the creation stories as etiological myths, we recognize that it was never the intention of the first two chapters of Genesis to describe *how* humanity or anything else came to exist. Rather, it was the intention of those texts to describe *why* humanity came to exist. The answer to how humanity has come to exist is the job of the natural sciences and reason; the question belongs to the immanent dimension of reality. The answer to why humanity has come to exist is the job of theology and faith; it belongs to the transcendent dimension of reality. It is the purview of the natural sciences to determine how, when, and where Homo sapiens developed, but not why. It is the purview of theology to propose the why, the purpose of humanity.

The continuum of all that exists in the universe that physics proposes does not diminish the unique dignity of humanity from the theological viewpoint. The Old Testament muses on the question of the special character of humanity that sets it apart from the rest of creation. The first two chapters of Genesis express both that people are very much parts of the greater whole that is creation and that we have a unique character that distinguishes us from everything else.

The first story of creation in the first chapter of Genesis was written by the Priestly source (P), probably as a hymn to be used in the Temple of Jerusalem. God creates humanity, which in Hebrew is *'adam,* on the sixth day of the seven-day week, on the same day and in the same way as "the cattle and creeping things and wild animals of the earth of every kind" (Gen 1:24). *'Adam* was not someone's name in ancient Hebrew; it just meant humankind. P understands us as creatures in line with all the other creatures God creates. But the author also thinks that people have a special character and role in creation. Humanity is the only creature made "in the image and likeness of God" (Gen 1:27). We are symbols of God in a way no other creature is. We make God present in an extraordinary way; God works through us in a unique way. God charges us to be fruitful and multiply, and to fill the earth and subdue it and to have dominion over the rest of creation (Gen 1:28). Scripture scholars interpret "subdue" and "have dominion over" to mean that the author saw humanity as taking an active and forceful role in directing creation. Scripture scholar Richard J. Clifford proposes that the Hebrew word for subdue, *kabas,* has the nuance of "to master," "to bring forcefully under control." He continues: "Force is necessary at the beginning to make the untamed land serve humans. Humans nonetheless are to respect the environment; they are not to kill for food but are to treat all life with respect."[24] The text foresees people as rulers but not abusers.[25] This is the theme of Pope Francis's beautiful encyclical *Laudato Si'.* The entire creation has been made through the Word of God by the power of God's Breath; people are the crown of that creation. The author (P) emphasizes this distinction by God's words at the end of the sixth day. Unlike days one to five, which are described as "good," now God says that everything he had made was "very good" (Gen 1:31). The

---

[24] Richard J. Clifford, "Genesis," *The New Jerome Biblical Commentary* (Englewood Cliffs, NJ: Prentice Hall, 1990), 2:5.

[25] S. Wagner, "*kabas, kebes; kibsan,*" in *Theological Dictionary of the Old Testament,* vol. 7, ed. G. Johannes Botterweck, Heinz-Josef Fabry, and Helmer Ringren (Grand Rapids, MI: Eerdmans, 1995), 52–57.

story concludes with the sabbath. As Abraham Heschel writes in his moving, meditative book *The Sabbath: Its Meaning for Modern Man*,[26] the sabbath represents the culmination of creation for which Jews yearn. The weekly celebration of the sabbath is an inchoate experience of heaven in which humanity participates in the rest (*shabbat* in Hebrew), and the peace and completeness *(shalom)* of God.

The second story of creation begins with the second part of Genesis 2:4. The literary source has changed from Priestly to Yahwist (J). The J source is full of pastoral imagery, which leads scholars to suppose the source came from farmers. The scene is desolate until God creates humanity; J uses the same word here, *'adam*, as P did. The story is full of sublime symbolism. Our farmer, J, describes a very anthropomorphic God who bends down to the ground, forms a human figure out of clay, and breathes life into it. J expresses the insight that people belong to the earth that J farmed, and that the principle of life that animates that earth is God himself. J goes on to paint the picture of the most beautiful farm he can imagine: the Garden of Eden. He fills it with everything he imagines the perfect farm would have: water, plants, and animals. He entrusts the whole to humankind, instructing us to use it for our own benefit. He also warns us against trying to be gods ourselves by eating of the tree of life and the tree of the knowledge "of good and evil" (Gen 2:17). Good and evil is a merism, a literary technique that expresses a whole by speaking of the two extremes contained in that whole: I worked from the minute I got up to the minute I went to bed, that is, I worked all day. The warnings against eating from the trees is a warning to be who we are, finite humans, and not to try to be what we are not, that is, infinite. God creates the animals out of the ground to be *'adam*'s "helper and partner" (Gen 2:18). God creates them just as he did *'adam*, but there is no mention of breathing the divine principle of life into them. *'Adam* names all the

---

[26] Abraham Joshua Heschel, *The Sabbath: Its Meaning for Modern Man* (New York: Farrar, Straus, and Young, 1951).

animals, signifying his authority over them, but he has been warned not to harm them.

I'm always amused by the story of the creation of the woman after the animals. The author observes that the human being lacked something: "for *'adam* there was not found a helper as his partner" (Gen 2:20). It's as if a little light goes off in the divine brain as God looks upon a somewhat lonely *'adam* and gets the message that pets are nice, but. . . . So God gets the bright idea to create "a woman." The formation of the woman (*'ishah* in Hebrew) from the rib of *'adam* beautifully expresses J's understanding of the unity, and therefore the desire for unity, of the sexes. *'Adam* approves of the divine handiwork with a shriek of joy, naming the woman *'ishah* because she came out of *'ish*, a man. Where are we going in J's eyes? Toward unity.

Chapters 3 to 11 retell a series of stories that recount how people succumb to the temptation to evil. These are the stories of Adam and Eve eating the forbidden fruit, of Cain murdering his brother Abel, of licentious behavior that brought on the Great Flood, and of the pride at the tower of Babel. The story of creation that had started out so promisingly takes a turn for the worse. Discord rears its ugly head in paradise.

Christian theology, especially under the influence of the great church father Saint Augustine in the fourth and fifth centuries, sees these stories as telling us about the "fall" of humankind. Adam and Eve committed the "original sin," which, according to Augustine, has been passed down from generation to generation through the concupiscence that is associated with making new generations. Augustine proposed that everyone who engages in procreation does so for at least some selfish reason. Adam and Eve disfigured the image of God in humanity. We are no longer purely altruistic and loving but also selfish and hateful.

Augustine's observation that we are a mixture of altruism and selfishness is right on the money. As discussed above, science proves that he was right. Altruism and selfishness are characteristics that fuel evolution. Poor Augustine, however, did not have the advantage of being familiar with Charles

Darwin, who lived in the nineteenth century, and his theory of evolution. Nor was Augustine familiar with literary criticism of the Bible. If he had been, he would have known that the first eleven chapters of the Book of Genesis are all etiological myths and that there really were no individual people named Adam, Eve, Cain, Abel, Noah and his family, and the people who built the tower of Babel.

Darwin and literary criticism change the origin but not the character of original sin. We are, indeed, born with altruistic and selfish instincts that, thanks to conscience, put us into very uncomfortable positions. If we use our conscience, we can all identify with Saint Paul when he cries out: "For I do not do the good I want, but the evil I do not want is what I do" (Rom 7:19). We do so not because two people, Adam and Eve, sinned and passed that sin down through the generations, but rather because we are made that way. This condition is what Daryl Domning renames "original selfishness."[27] He, with Saint Paul, proposes that the only release—or "ransom"—is through the death and resurrection of Jesus Christ. Through baptism we die and rise with Christ through the Holy Spirit. We then have the responsibility to cooperate with God and with one another in completing what is lacking in the suffering of Christ. We labor with Christ, we minister with Christ, for the salvation of the world.

A Paradigm for Church:
A Synthesis of Immanent and Transcendent

We have gazed at the reality of our universe through the eyes of science and revelation. We're looking for clues that can help us identify the church's identity and the roles that its members should assume to promote the evolution of salvation history.

---

[27] Daryl P. Domning and Monika Hellwig, *Original Selfishness: Original Sin and Evil in the Light of Evolution* (Burlington, VT: Ashgate, 2006).

In light of the data from science and faith, what paradigm will we develop for thinking about the church and for its organization such that everyone actively participates in its life and work? The data, though very different, reveal patterns that are remarkably similar. Both help us to understand what the church is and, consequently, the roles people play in the church.

Physics identifies the increased organization and complexity of matter under the influence of an infusion of energy. It also recognizes that the infusion of energy into one system means the depletion of energy in another, and thus a decrease in organization and complexity of matter. Faith perceives the transcendent significance of the increase in complexity and organization in the universe. Teilhard muses on this significance at the end of *The Human Phenomenon*. He associates the rise of consciousness or conscience (the word is the same in French) with the increased complexity of matter and its "enfolding" of itself, as mentioned above. He proposes that if we are to understand humanity we must recognize our place within the "convergent cosmic atmosphere."[28]

Human work can be morally good or bad depending on whether it contributes to and participates in God's creative work throughout the universe. The human conscience is able to perceive what activity does and what does not contribute to and participate in this process. All human work, energized by the Holy Spirit, that cooperates with God is ministry; all that does not is sinful and, therefore, destructive. Human work energized by the Holy Spirit effectively harnesses immanent energy—the immanent manifestation of the transcendent Holy Spirit. Following the laws of physics it participates in evolution. In and of itself, of course, evolution has no morality. Morality appears only with conscience. People who follow their conscience do their best to be co-creators with God. They contribute to bringing creation beyond selfishness into fulfillment in heaven. There we join with the author of the Book of Revelation in proclaiming:

---

[28] Teilhard de Chardin, *The Human Phenomenon*, 218.

"See, the home of God is among mortals.
He will dwell with them;
they will be his peoples,
and God himself will be with them;
he will wipe every tear from their eyes.
Death will be no more;
mourning and crying and pain will be no
        more,
for the first things have passed away."

And the one who was seated on the throne said, "See, I am making all things new." (Rev 21:3–5)

Using the eyes of faith, therefore, we propose that what we call energy in the immanent dimension of reality that was released in the Big Bang is a manifestation of the transcendent Holy Spirit. The immanent matter that has been forming, converging, and becoming more organized is a manifestation of the Son. The Father speaks the Son, the eternal Word, through whom the Father creates by the power of the Holy Spirit. The universe is charged with the presence of God and, as Augustine was fond of noting, all creation bears the footprint, the *vestigium*, of the Trinity. Evolution is the process by which creation develops more and more into the communion that it really is. Teilhard situated creation within the incarnate Son, who is the Alpha and the Omega of the universe. We might think of the Big Bang as the universe's Alpha and the universe's death as the Omega. In that Omega we join Christ in his transformative death, the passage empowered by the Holy Spirit of love, to resurrection and eternal communion with the eternal Community.

Chapter 2

Church and Ministry in Scripture

As we saw in Chapter 1, we humans are a product of the interplay between energy and matter that drives evolution. Through genetic mutation, natural selection, and biocultural evolution we have developed into a eusocial species. *Eusocial* is a relative newcomer (1966) to the English language. It refers to behavior with very high levels of cooperative socialization. Among the members of this elite group are, as we saw in the previous chapter, bees, ants, and . . . people.[1] Our consciences urge us to promote more altruism and to eschew selfishness. As a result of this instinctual urge toward eusociality we organize ourselves into eusocial groups such as families, clans, tribes, and nations. Social scientists demonstrate that kin relationship

---

[1] See further E. O. Wilson and B. Hölldobler, "Eusociality: Origin and Consequences," *Proceedings of the National Academy of Sciences of the USA* 102 (2005): 13367–71; M. A. Nowak, Corina E. Tarnita, and Edward O. Wilson, "The Evolution of Eusociality," *Nature* 466 (2010): 1057–62; Samuel Bowles and Herbert Gintis, *A Cooperative Species: Human Reciprocity and Its Evolution* (Princeton, NJ: Princeton University Press), 2011; Joan E. Strassmann, David C. Queller, John C. Avise, and Francisco J. Ayala, "In the Light of Evolution V: Cooperation and Conflict," *Proceedings of the National Academy of Sciences of the United States of America* (June 28, 2011) 108 (Supplement 2): 10787–89; Martin A. Nowak with Roger Highfield, *Super-Cooperators: Altruism, Evolution and Why We Need Each Other to Succeed* (New York: Free Press, 2011); Edward O. Wilson, *The Social Conquest of Earth* (New York: Norton, 2012).

is not the deciding factor in this organization. Blood is thicker than water may be a common saying, but we tend to act just as selflessly for people to whom we are not related. There is an evolutionary advantage to extending eusociality beyond just family. It makes sense to have allies or friends who have our back beyond just siblings and cousins. This is why clubs, neighborhoods, clans, tribes, and nations form and thrive. Theological reflection upon this immanent phenomenon leads us to perceive the transcendent hand of God here.[2] God is a Trinity, a communion of perfectly altruistic love. We are the image of God. Despite contemporary emphases on individuality and individualism, it is humanity as a whole that Genesis describes as being made in the image and likeness of God. That includes, of course, each individual member of humanity. Indeed, as we will see below, humanity itself is catholic. God is present in the whole and in the parts.

The Formation of the Church

As I said in Chapter 1, theology's interpretation of the immanent data from natural and social science sees the transcendent creative act of God in evolution. We see God infusing all of creation, from subatomic particles to galaxies, with the animation that is the Holy Spirit. That energy, whether seen from the immanent or transcendent perspective, organizes the stuff of the universe into more complex systems while at the same time leaving a wake of entropy or disorganization. Organization and chaos, life and death, are dance partners as evolution proceeds on its merry way. It is in the context of this microscopic and macroscopic dance that we must situate what Christians call the church and ministry.

---

[2] See Paul Rigby and Paul O'Grady, "Agape and Altruism: Debates in Theology and Social Psychology," *Journal of the American Academy of Religion* 57 (1989): 719–37.

When did the church begin and what, exactly, is it? There is no lack of variety in answers offered by theologians over the centuries. Thomas Aquinas dates the birth of the church to Abel. A popular traditional starting point for the church has often been Pentecost, as described in the Acts of the Apostles, or perhaps when Christ breathed the Holy Spirit on the disciples in the Gospel of John. Those are neat answers, but life is rarely neat. The Vatican II document *Lumen gentium*, also known as the *Dogmatic Constitution on the Church*, adopts the model of the people of God, that is, people whom God chooses, to describe the church. It must, however, acknowledge that if trademarks existed in the ancient world, that name already had been taken by the Israelites. The council documents recognize this potential "trademark violation" when it writes: "Israel according to the flesh, which wandered as an exile in the desert, was already called the Church of God" (*LG* 9). Avery Dulles appreciates the value of this way of thinking of the church but expresses a little theological discomfort. He wonders if its use may strike some as egotistical and monopolistic.[3] If the Christian Church is the people of God, who is everybody else? This applies especially to the Jews who, after all, did have first dibs on the expression.

The council document refers to a number of uses of the Hebrew word *qahal* here to support its point (see Neh 13:1; cf. Deut 23:1 ff.; Num 20:4). This Hebrew word, which essentially means an assembly of people, has a fairly specific use in the Old Testament. The Old Testament frequently qualifies the word to identify its purpose: there are assemblies for all kinds of things from worship to politics to war. In Deuteronomy 5:22 the word describes the assembly of the Israelites who receive the Decalogue, that is, the Ten Commandments, the Torah, or the Law, and are called the people of God.

---

[3] Avery Dulles, *Models of the Church* (New York: Doubleday, 1987), 47–62.

This special designation for the assembly becomes a standard phrase in Hebrew: the *qahal Yahweh*.[4] In the Hebrew version of the Book of Sirach, one of the younger books of the Old Testament, *qahal* is practically equivalent to a city-state as understood by the ancient Greeks.[5] In the period after the Old Testament it sometimes referred to synagogues, which were and are places for people to assemble as the people of God.[6] It is important here to recall that the ancient world did not distinguish between sacred and secular in the same way that we do today. Sure there were occasions, places, and activities that promoted stronger transcendent experiences than others. These would be the equivalent of us listening to music or going to a movie and being transported somewhere else—not in the sense that our bodies levitate (though if the music or the movie is really good, it will have a somatic effect) but in the sense of sensing the presence of God in a particularly powerful way. God, however, is actually equally present everywhere.

An ancient translation of the Old Testament into Greek, the Septuagint, probably composed in the third century BCE, uses the Greek word *ekklesía* to translate the Hebrew word *qahal*. *Ekklesía* is a compound word in Greek, formed by *ek + kaleo*, literally, "to call out." The word conjures up our experiences of being called or invited to join a club, team, or any group. It's a wonderful feeling to be called out of being alone and to be a part of something social. This sense of belonging would have been particularly meaningful to the Israelites who drew so much of their identity from their national, social network. The Greek word eventually wandered over to Latin, where it became *ecclesia*, the basis for all Romance language words for church.

---

[4] "*Qahal*" in *Theological Dictionary of the Old Testament*, vol. 12, ed. G. Johannes Botterweck, Heinz-Josef Fabry, and Helmer Ringgren (Grand Rapids, MI: Eerdmans, 2012), 553.

[5] Ibid., 559.

[6] Ibid.

The New Testament used the Greek word *ekklesía* to refer to the Christian community.[7] Modern translations into English generally use the word *church* to translate *ekklesía*. Exactly what *ekklesía* or "Christian community" meant to the followers of Jesus in the first century is more complicated than at first meets the eye. In his insightful work *The Churches the Apostles Left Behind*,[8] the great scripture scholar Raymond Brown demonstrates that first-century Christians had very, very diverse understandings of what the *ekklesía*, the Christian community, the church, was and how it was organized. This diversity gives witness to the rich variety by which Christians have, and can, think of the church and how members of the church have and can contribute to its life.

In light of the Bible's descriptions of how the Israelites and the first Christians understood themselves, and how Vatican II recognizes the existence of the church in Old Testament Israel, we may be able to assuage Avery Dulles's theological discomfort about adopting the model of people of God for the church. Why limit people of God only to Jews and Christians? Thomas Aquinas didn't! Is there anyone or any group on earth whom God does not choose? Is anyone or any group *not* the people of God? And while we're at it, in light of the seamless connection we've seen by looking at creation as evolving from the Big Bang through the interplay of energy and matter, the Holy Spirit, and the Son, why not include all of creation within the church?

The Holy Spirit and the Son permeate(s) all creation. The Book of Daniel describes the three faithful Jews in Nebuchadnezzar's furnace calling upon every single creature to bless God (3:51–90). Saint Francis of Assisi's *Canticle of the Sun* calls upon God to be praised in all creatures. Pope Francis's encyclical *Laudato si'*, whose title is taken from Saint Francis's

---

[7] K. L. Schmidt, "Ekklesia," in *Theological Dictionary of the New Testament*, vol. 3, ed. Gerhard Kittel (Grand Rapid, MI: Eerdmans, 1965), 529.

[8] Raymond E. Brown, SS, *The Churches the Apostles Left Behind* (Mahwah, NJ: Paulist Press, 1984).

Canticle, rejoices in the interconnectedness of all creation and calls for an anthropology that recognizes humanity's proper role in creation. Teilhard's *The Human Phenomenon* radiates awe in describing the seamless progression of the evolution of energy and matter that culminates in humanity: stardust animated by the Holy Spirit. Let us welcome all creation into the *ekklesía*, called out of disorder into community with God. The church understood in this way becomes the universal icon of the Trinity. As Bruno Forte describes, it is

> the sacrament, that is the sign and chosen instrument, of the divine plan of unity, which goes from creation to the Parousia. The church is the historical participation in trinitarian unity, the realization begun under the veil of signs of salvation gushing forth from the divine initiative, the mystery or sacrament "of the intimate union with God and the unity of all humankind."[9]

Recognizing that all creation is part of the church, called by God into participation in Trinitarian unity, helps us to appreciate the true catholicity of the church. We can marvel at its seemingly infinite diversity, ever changing while remaining the same: icon of the Trinity. We can appreciate the diverse ways by which every single entity contributes to the good of the whole. And we can zoom forward to the appearance of humankind to value the contributions, the ministries, of every human being to the life of the community.

The Church with a Human Face

In 1985 the Flemish Dominican theologian Edward Schillebeeckx published a book in Dutch that was translated into

---

[9] Bruno Forte, *La chiesa icona della Trinità. Breve ecclesiologia.* Universale teologica 9 (Brescia: Queriniana, 1984), 18; interior quotation is from *LG* 1.

a variety of more popular languages. In English it was given the title *The Church with a Human Face*.[10] Translations are always approximations and interpretations. The English title is not at all a literal translation of the original, but it does tell us what the book is about. A literal translation of the original title would be something like *A Plea for People in the Church: Christian Identity and Ministries in the Church*. Schilleebeckx recognizes that humanity is an integral part of God's work of creation, writing, "Men and women are co-creators of the kingdom of God."[11]

As we have seen, everything in the universe participates in God's work of creation as energy organizes matter. More organized systems, ones we call life, can even manipulate how energy organizes matter. And the most complex systems, those that are conscious, do so by making choices that affect what they become. Through biocultural evolution we humans direct who we become by expressing ourselves. This self-expression, literally "pressing ourselves out," affects not only who we become but, to an unprecedented degree among all other physical open systems, what happens to the rest of the planet on which we live—and maybe beyond. From the theological perspective this self-expression is the response to our vocation. God calls the universe into being through the Word and the Holy Spirit. What we do with our lives is our response to that call. The response to our vocation makes us more and more human. Our work is a cooperation with God in directing creation toward its fulfillment in the community of the Trinity. The church that began with the Big Bang assumes a human face through activity. The work that people do, the utilization of energy, affects the universe's evolutionary trajectory. Work that promotes salvation, that answers the divine vocation, is ministry.

---

[10] Edward Schillebeeckx, *Pleidooi voor mensen in de kerk. Christelijke identiteit en ambten in de kerk* (Baarn: Nelissen, 1985). In English, *The Church with a Human Face* (New York: Crossroad, 1985).

[11] Schillebeeckx, *The Church with a Human Face*, 19.

The Christian tradition, as evidenced by the above-quoted statement from *Lumen gentium*, flows directly from the Jewish tradition. In fact, it thinks of itself as a continuation of the story or the history of salvation that constitutes the Jewish tradition. This is not to say that the history of salvation began with and is limited to the Jewish tradition. God certainly appears to have been busy creating and drawing creation toward fulfillment throughout the universe in general and in people all over the world in particular. The church is catholic, after all.

Vatican II's *Dogmatic Constitution on Divine Revelation (Dei verbum)* teaches that God gives people "an enduring witness to Himself in created realities (see Rom 1:19–20)." Planning to make known the way of heavenly salvation, He went further and from the start manifested Himself to our first parents" (*DV* 3), to the original Hebrews (*DV* 3), and ultimately in Christ, the fullness of his revelation. The Christian tradition recognizes the tremendous wisdom of the writers of what we Christians call the Old Testament. *Dei verbum* expresses the confidence we put into the whole Bible: "The books of Scripture must be acknowledged as teaching solidly, faithfully, and without error that truth which God wanted put into the sacred writings for the sake of salvation" (*DV* 11). It's important to draw attention to the explanation of the Bible's freedom from error. The Bible's texts faithfully express what God wants us to know to help us evolve toward salvation. Let's take a look at the texts for insights into the church.

The Church in Scripture

The people of Israel understood themselves as existing as a people thanks to God's vocation. They grew to recognize that although they were the chosen people, God also chooses all humankind. We see this most clearly in the story of the covenant God made with Noah, who was not a Hebrew. Israel begins its national and cultural history of salvation with Abraham. The Book of Deuteronomy, written to reinvigorate the people's faith and fervor, wants the people to remember how they came to be:

> A wandering Aramean was my ancestor; he went down into Egypt and lived there as an alien, few in number, and there he become a great nation, mighty and populous. . . . The Lord heard our voice and saw our affliction, our toil, and our oppression. The Lord brought us out of Egypt with a mighty hand and an outstretched arm, with a terrifying display of power, and with signs and wonders; and he brought us into this place and gave us this land, a land flowing with milk and honey. (Deut 26:5–9)

The text urges the Israelites to recognize themselves as the chosen people, the people of God. It wants them to experience themselves and all they possess as gifts of God. It challenges them to ask what their appropriate response should be. The answer is provided in the text that Jews universally recognize as foundational for their culture: "Hear, O Israel, the Lord is our God, the Lord alone. You shall love the Lord your God with all your heart, and with all your soul, and with all your might" (Deut 6:4–5). Jews call this text the *Shema*, from its first word, which means "hear." The Book of Deuteronomy wants people to remember it and so orders them to hang it just about everywhere, including their doorposts and foreheads. Only Orthodox Jews follow the complete instructions literally, but most Jews do put the text in a little box called a *mezuzah* and attach it to their doorpost so they are reminded of it every time they pass by. In the New Testament Jesus reprises this foundational text and combines it with another from the Book of Leviticus (17:18) in what we often call the Great Commandment. The fundamental, primordial act for human beings is love of God and love of neighbor (Mark 12:28–31; cf. Matt 22:34–40; Luke 10:25–28). Luke's parable of the Good Samaritan makes it clear that neighbor means everyone. In the concluding exercise of Ignatius Loyola's *Spiritual Exercises*, called the "Contemplación Para Alcanzar Amor" (contemplation to attain God's love), he writes that love ought to manifest itself in deeds rather than in words, and love consists in a mutual sharing.[12] To be human, to advance salvation history, every single person must express love in action by sharing. This sharing includes one's talents.

The history of Israel, insofar as we can piece it together from the Old Testament, gives evidence of a slow, unsteady yet clear evolution of the people's self-consciousness of the significance of their identity as the chosen people. At first they understood their status as distinctive; that is, they were chosen by God and other people were not. This gave them the right to conquer Palestine and slaughter its inhabitants. Later, however, they recognized themselves as chosen to be light to the nations. Their national egotism gives signs of realizing that God loves all people, indeed all creation, and that God is the God, the ultimate goal, of all people, whether or not they are aware of it. Christians see this process fulfilled in the New Testament through the Jews. The opening of the doors to the Gentiles, the non-Jews, that we witness especially in the Gospel of Matthew, the Acts of the Apostles, and the epistles of Paul gives us a picture of what the early church looked like. It was united into the one body of Christ, which its members described as animated by the same Holy Spirit throughout. It was holy because of its association with the incarnate Son. It was catholic in its makeup, with people from all kinds of cultures, walks of life, and talents who worked together synergistically for the common good. And it was apostolic as it reached out to the whole world to share the gospel, the faith fully revealed in Christ that gathers all human cultures into the same project of cooperating with God to bring salvation history to fulfillment.[13]

The Holy Spirit energizes matter, organizing it more and more into the body of the Son, Christ. New Testament writers

---

[12] Ignatius Loyola, *The Spiritual Exercises*, trans. Luis J. Puhl, SJ (New York: Random House, 2000), annotation 230–31.

[13] See further the work of Jacques Dupuis, SJ, especially *Jesus Christ at the Encounter of World Religions* (Maryknoll, NY: Orbis Books, 1991) and *Toward a Christian Theology of Religious Pluralism* (Maryknoll, NY: Orbis Books, 2001).

attribute to the Holy Spirit the reason for life. From the perspective of science this corresponds to the increased complexity of matter and the development of eusociality. Paul muses on creation's labor pains under the impulse of the Holy Spirit, forming all of humanity into the Body of Christ (Rom 8), in which each member has talents for work (1 Cor 12). Luke's story of Pentecost (Acts 2) sees the Holy Spirit as infusing energy into all people. The Spirit gathers people together in a reversal of the cacophony that resulted from the sin at the tower of Babel (Gen 11). Now all people understand one another. All people can communicate, collaborate, cooperate. They can overcome selfishness. In John's description of the commissioning of the first disciples the resurrected Jesus appears in a locked upper room to people who are hiding. He encourages them. He wishes them peace—dynamic confidence that comes from communion with God. He shows them his wounds, that is, the necessity to die to selfishness in order to pass to a new life of altruism. He sends them to continue and to fulfill the same mission that he received from the Father. The disciples become an extension of Christ, working in the world. He then gives them the Holy Spirit to forgive sins (John 20). This act is a reprise of Jesus's gifts from the cross, when he breathed his Spirit on the disciples gathered below (John 19:30) and when blood and water poured forth from his pierced side (John 19:34). The Holy Spirit is divine energy, the same energy that has been bringing matter together since the Big Bang. The Spirit is also the same energy that, through the very gathering of matter, promotes death. The energy that organizes matter is dispersed. Theology equates this entropy with death, which, in the cross of Christ, is the means of resurrection. It is liberation from the sinful structures that characterize human eusociality. The cross is the truth that sets us free.

The effect of the outpouring of the Holy Spirit and of the blood and water from Jesus's pierced side, as described in John's Gospel, is to advance a process that the Bible sees having started with the call of Abraham in the Book of Genesis. The stories of the fall preceding those of Abraham are, as we have already seen, all various myths to describe human selfishness, human sinfulness. Abraham is the first person described in Genesis who actually listens to God. He obeys. He allows God to infuse him with the power to complete the human pilgrimage from sinfulness to sanctity. That process consists in gathering desperate, sinful people into ever-more-eusocial groups. The offspring of Abraham and Sarah are portrayed as working together, in fits and starts, to build the nation. Sometimes they seem to take two steps forward and one step back. The prophets spoke the word, criticizing them for being backsliders. Sometimes they listened; sometimes they didn't. Disobedience was always followed by disaster, brought on by the refusal to live through the Holy Spirit.

As explained above, the most common term for the community of Christians in the New Testament is the Greek word *ekklesía*. Like *qahal* in the Old Testament, *ekklesía* was just a common term for an assembly of people in ancient Greek. Again like *qahal*, it could just as easily refer to a political entity as people who came together to pray. The New Testament thinks of the *ekklesía* as the continuation of the *qahal* of Israel. The word conveys a very concrete reality: real people who come together because they feel drawn by Christ. At the same time it conveys a sense of mystery: each individual assembly of people drawn together by Christ is the *ekklesía* and so is the collective of assemblies the *ekklesía*.[14] Although the word *ekklesía* is translated into English variously as "congregation" and "assembly," its most common rendering in English is "church."[15]

As Raymond Brown demonstrated, the early Christians had a catholic understanding of the church. How they organized the

---

[14] See Raimund Köbert, "qhl (pal.-aram) - *ekklesia*," in *Biblica* 46 (1965): 464.

[15] M. H. Pope, "Congregation, Assembly," *The Interpreter's Dictionary of the Bible* (New York: Abingdon Press, 1962), 669–70. The English word *church* comes to us through Dutch (*kerk*) and German (*Kirche*) from the Greek expression *kuriakon doma*: "the house belonging to the Lord."

assembly always developed with respect to historical contexts. This is very important: there was no uniform understanding or organization for the church. The various ways of understanding and organizing the church sprang from Christians' experience of the Holy Spirit in their everyday lives. They were ways of promoting the life of the church in specific situations, faced with specific challenges, with respect to their faith in Christ. Like everything else in the world, they developed according to the laws of evolution. Some of the ways by which they organized themselves fared better than others in the process of natural selection. We'll draw upon Brown's scholarship to look at the church in the first and second centuries in order to draw lessons about the value and character of the work they inspired.[16]

The Pauline tradition in the letters to the Corinthians, Ephesians, and Colossians imagines the church as the very body of Christ, of which Christ is the head. Christ's presence in the *ekklesía*, however, is not limited to the head: Christ is present in the whole body.[17] Each member of the body has his or her own gifts or talents to contribute to the life of the body. None is more highly valued than others. If anything, those whom some might consider less honorable are accorded greater honor in the church (1 Cor 12:22–25). The later letters to Timothy and Titus, known as the Pastoral Epistles, describe a structure of overseers *(episkopoi)*, elders *(presbuteroi)*, and deacons *(diakonoi)* in the church, but this structure is not found in all the small assembles we read about in the New Testament. There is no evidence that these people had any leadership role in the liturgy. They were, rather, teachers, representatives of the community, and administrators. These were ministries that, among other tasks, sorted through what people were claiming

---

[16] Brown, *The Churches the Apostles Left Behind*. See also Raymond Brown, *Priest and Bishop: Biblical Reflections* (Paramus, NJ: Paulist Press, 1970); Bernard P. Robinson, "Patterns of Ministry in the New Testament Church," *New Blackfriars* 83 (2002): 73–85.

[17] Brown, *The Churches the Apostles Left Behind*, 47ff.; Schmidt, "*Ekklesia*," 529.

to be divine revelation to see whether or not those claims were authentic. Bishops and presbyters seem to have been two names for people who did the same thing. They sorted through the sense of the faithful and kept order in the community. The Pastoral Epistles provide no evidence that these ministers did anything else, such as presiding at liturgies.

James 5:14 assigns the anointing of the sick to *presbyters*, the Greek word for elders. Elders had played the role of authority figures for centuries in Israel. James here is referring not to someone holding an office but to someone with a traditional role of leadership within the community, something like the head of a household.[18] Presbyters did not anoint the sick on their own authority but as a leader and representative of the community. It is the whole community who prays for the sick person, led by the presbyter.[19] The presbyter exercises the ministry of leadership, facilitating the community's communal prayer.

Women are mentioned in the context of the qualifications for deacons in 1 Timothy 3:11, though it is not clear if the author is referring to women who were deacons. Romans 16:1, however, explicitly refers to a woman, Phoebe, as a "*diakonos* of the *ekklesía* at Cenchreae." It does so to describe her as someone who helps Paul and many other people. It is unclear whether or not her role was part of some greater organizational structure. The development of the structure described in the Pastoral Epistles was in response to the need for organization in the assembly. This particular way of organizing the assembly was not at first universal or even uniform. It caught on because it worked well in those circumstances: an example of natural selection.

---

[18] Patrick Hartin, *James*, Sacra Pagina 14 (Collegeville, MN: Liturgical Press, 2003), 267.

[19] Ibid., 274–77; Daniel R. Hayden, "Calling the Elders to Pray," *Bibliotheca Sacra* 138 (1981): 258–66. See further Günther Bornkamm, "*Presbyter*," in *Theological Dictionary of the New Testament*, vol. 6 (Grand Rapids, MI: Eerdmans, 1968), 651–83.

The Acts of the Apostles describes the church as a continuation of the life and work of Christ in the disciples. We might think of Acts as Part 2 of the Gospel of Luke, written to deal with the somewhat unsettling realization that the end of the world wasn't as imminent as everyone thought. After the disciples had experienced Jesus's resurrection, they believed that Jesus would usher in a new age, the fulfillment of salvation history. It took them a while to come to grips with the fact that the dawn of the new age wasn't happening as they had imagined it would. Acts envisions the new age developing as the gospel is preached through the disciples, empowered as they are by the Holy Spirit. It, too, is aware of the existence of overseers and elders whose roles, as in the Pastoral Epistles, are not described as liturgical. The Acts of the Apostles never uses the noun *deacon*, but it does use the verb *diakoneo* to describe the charitable work that people did. While it describes the work of a group of people, it does not imply that other people's work was not also a function of their participation in the church.

The first letter of Peter offers more insight into the varied ways in which the Christian assemblies thought of themselves. The letter was written to a group of people who felt cut off from the rest of the great church. Its intention was to shore up their spirits and hope. The letter assumes the organizational structure outlined in the Pastoral Epistles; the author refers to himself as a presbyter (1 Pet 5:1). He urges his readers to think of themselves as heirs to the Israelites, whom God had freed from slavery in Egypt and who had wandered in the desert and journeyed to the Promised Land. The parallel and encouragement crescendo:

> But you are a chosen race, a royal priesthood, a holy nation, God's own people, in order that you may proclaim the mighty acts of him who calls you out of darkness into his marvelous light. (1 Pet 2:9)

This passage is the only one in the New Testament to apply a form of the word *priest (hiereus)* to Christians. The only other time the New Testament uses the word, except in reference to the Jewish priesthood, is when it is applied to Christ in the Letter to the Hebrews. It is important to keep in mind that first-century Christians did not think of any member of their assembly as a priest. Rather, they thought of themselves as participating in Christ's priesthood. The main function of Jewish priests at the time of Jesus was to offer sacrifice. Christ was a priest because he offered *the* sacrifice: himself. We generally think of a sacrifice as giving something away. Its root meaning, however, is "to make holy" *(sacer + facere)*. The Greek word for priest expresses the same connection with holiness; *hiereus* is "priest" and *hieros* is "holy." All Christians, according to 1 Peter, participate in Christ's activity as a priest. Their entire lives, including all the work they do, is to be directed to making the world holy by sacrificing themselves, by giving themselves away in love.

Matthew is the only Gospel to use the word *ekklesía*. It does so twice: in Matthew 16:18 and in Matthew 18. Matthew uses the word in order to emphasize the fulfillment of the Hebrew *ekklesía* in the assembly of Christians. Matthew 16:18 describes the foundation of the *ekklesía* on Peter, the leader of the disciples, and gives him authority to develop the church as he sees fit. The conferral of the keys is a reference to the authority given to the prime minister in the dynasty of King David in Isaiah 22:22. As the prime minister exercises the king's power, so Peter has authority to direct the *ekklesía*. The other use of *ekklesía* in Matthew's Gospel is in the context of a speech by Jesus to those with pastoral authority in the church. Matthew thinks of Jesus as a kind of new Moses: a lawgiver. It's not by accident that Matthew, but not Luke, situates Jesus's great sermon on a mount. He wishes to draw a parallel between the Law of Moses and that of Jesus. Rather than give a specific code of laws to follow, however, Jesus tries to instruct the leaders in how to think through problems. The emphasis is not on authority but on the wisdom that should guide the authorities. Brown comments:

The one evangelist to use the word "church" and to speak of Jesus's building or founding the church understood the possibility that the church might become a self-sufficient entity, ruling (in the name of Christ, to be sure) by its own authority, its own teaching, and its own commandments.[20]

The wisdom that would guide the church in facing changing circumstances includes the wisdom to craft new organizational systems adapted to the changing environments in which the church lives.

The church that developed around the Gospel of John and the three epistles of John demonstrated great wisdom but a lack of its application to practical challenges that faced the *ekklesía*. This community thought of itself as intimately united with Christ and animated by the Holy Spirit. It was charismatic, encouraging members to exercise their talents as they felt moved by the Spirit. The only law was the law of love. It must have been the first- and second-century version of the 1960s in North America and Europe. Trouble arose when different people claimed that the Holy Spirit had given them contradictory instructions, and there was no one in authority to mediate the conflicts. The church of John shines as a beacon to us of the importance of adherence to Christ and of inspiration by the Holy Spirit, whom John calls the advocate or counselor, but its lack of organizational structure destroyed it. The lesson for us is that not everyone can do everything. The community needs authorities to organize its members so that all put their talents to work for the advancement of salvation history.

The Biblical Understanding of Ministry

From our discussion of the *ekklesía* as described in the New Testament we must conclude that Jesus did not intend to found

---

[20] Brown, *The Churches the Apostles Left Behind*, 138.

a long-term organization called the church. It's most probable that he, too, thought that the end of the world was imminent. The *ekklesía* formed around him first as his disciples. Disciples are both students and people who teach what they have learned from their master.[21] Jesus's disciples were attracted to him by his charism, works, and wisdom. After his death and resurrection they felt inspired to proclaim what they had learned: the "good news" or "gospel" of the way to fulfillment and salvation. When the world stubbornly refused to end, a plethora of communities formed. Eventually these communities thought of themselves as one, holy, catholic, and apostolic. Jesus, however, did not leave any instructions for how the church should be organized.[22]

The biblical evidence for the beginning of some sort of organizational structure in the church is really the evidence for the beginning of what we now call ministry. There is no exact equivalent of the word *ministry* in the Bible. Our English word has acquired many meanings over the centuries. It started off from the Latin word *ministerium*, which was an "office" or "service" and wandered through time picking up ever more associations. Those include everything from administering sacraments to administering government offices.[23] Various English translations of the Bible are inconsistent in their use of *minister* and *ministry*. Meinert Grumm points out an increasing reluctance on the part of translators to use the words *minister* and *ministry* at all. He notes that the King James Version

---

[21] Dulles, *Models of the Church*, chap. 13.

[22] See Richard P. McBrien, *The Church: The Evolution of Catholicism* (New York: HarperCollins, 2008), 29–31; Raymond F. Collins, "Did Jesus Found the Church? Which Church?" *Louvain Studies* 21 (1996): 356–64; Anton Houtepen, "Evangelie, kerk, ambt. Theologische diagnose van de huidige ambtsproblematiek," *Tijdschrift voor Theologie* 19 (1979): 235–52. English translation: Lucas Grollenberg, ed., "Gospel, Church, Ministry: A Theological Diagnosis of Present-day Problems in the Ministry," *Minister? Pastor? Prophet? Grass-roots Leadership in the Churches* (New York: Crossroad, 1981), 21–40.

[23] "ministry, n.", *OED Online*, January 2018. Oxford University Press.

(Standard Version of 1611) uses the words seventy times; the Revised Standard Version of 1952 reduces that to thirty times; the New English Bible of 1970 uses it eleven times; and the Good News Bible (Today's English Version) of 1976 doesn't have the words at all.[24]

A consideration of what words in the original Hebrew and Greek texts of the Bible are frequently translated as "minister" or "ministry" will give us some sense of what the authors of those texts had in mind and help us to focus on the original meaning of those words. A word in the Hebrew Old Testament that is often translated as "minister" is *seret*. If we look at how it is used, we see that its basic meaning is performing some kind of service. It refers to all kinds of people, including foreigners, and extends also to heavenly beings, who perform various acts of service.[25] It can refer to service in the Temple or other kinds of rituals, but it is not limited to that use.

The words for "minister" and "ministry" vary in the Septuagint (LXX), the Greek translation begun in the third century BCE of books that Jews considered inspired by God. The Hebrew word *seret* is translated into Greek by a variety of words that range in meaning from service in a ritual to service as a baker.[26] The range of words that the LXX uses to translate the one Hebrew word *seret* indicates to us the range of meanings of *minister* and *ministry* in the Old Testament. The LXX thus confirms that the concept of ministry included but was certainly not limited to rituals.

In the New Testament, which, like the LXX, was written in Greek, we see an evolution of the use of words for ministry.

---

[24] Meinert Grumm, "Ministry: The Old Testament Background," *Currents in Theology and Mission* 16 (1989): 104.

[25] Karen Engelken, "Seret," in *Theological Dictionary of the Old Testament*, vol. 15 (Grand Rapids, MI: Eerdmans 2006), 503–14. See also G. Henton Davies, "'Minister' in the Old Testament," in *The Interpreters Dictionary of the Bible*, vol. 3 (Nashville, TN: Abingdon Press, 1962), 385–86.

[26] R. Meyer, "*leitourgeo*," in *Theological Dictionary of the New Testament*, vol. 4 (Grand Rapids, MI: Eerdmans), 215–25.

The LXX uses some form of the word *leitourgeo* about a hundred times, almost always in reference to service at a ritual. The New Testament used a form of that only nine times.[27] This is linked to an evolution in the understanding of the character of priesthood. Rituals in the Old Testament are associated with priests in one form or another and usually involve sacrifice. Priests in the Old Testament are intermediaries between God and humanity in general and the people of Israel in particular. The Letter to the Hebrews understands Christ as the high priest who completes all the sacrifices of the Old Testament. He fulfills the Old Testament priesthood and makes the church a priestly people. This priestly people collectively participates in Christ's priesthood and Christ's sacrifice. As a result, the writers of the New Testament had little need of the word *leitourgeo*.

The New Testament paints the picture of Jesus's understanding of ministry as service. It uses two words associated with service that are frequently translated into English as "ministry": *apostolleo* and *diakoneo*. *Apostolleo* means "to send"; it is at the origin of the English word *apostle,* which is another way of saying *missionary. Diakoneo* means "to serve"; it is at the origin of the English word *deacon,* a person who serves. Jesus is described as one who is sent by the Father to serve, and in turn he sends his disciples to do the same thing. The form of service in the church evolved according to the changing needs and circumstances of different times and places.

The first people whom we should think of as ministers in the New Testament were the group known as the Twelve. These were the men who literally accompanied Jesus in his public ministry. It's likely that the number twelve is symbolic and was meaningful to first-century Jews. For centuries after the tenth century BCE, civil war that split the twelve tribes of Israel into two kingdoms, writers in the Old Testament pined for a reunification. This is especially true after the destruction of the

---

[27] H. Strathmann, *"leitourgeo,"* in *Theological Dictionary of the New Testament,* vol. 4 (Grand Rapids, MI: Eerdmans, 1965), 226–31; Grumm, "Ministry," 105.

ten northern tribes in the eighth century BCE, with only the tribes of Judah and Benjamin left in the south. Jesus's assembly of twelve companions symbolized for first-century Jews the longed-for reconstitution of the ancient nation. This reconstitution had eschatological overtones; that is, it symbolized the dawn of the end times. It was thought that the reconstitution of Israel would be a sign and means for the establishment of the kingdom of God.

According to the Acts of the Apostles, the Twelve continued Jesus's ministry and exercised certain administrative responsibilities in the primitive church. Nevertheless, their mission was not substantially different from that of other members of the community.[28] The group was not renewed after Matthias replaced Judas, as described in the Acts of the Apostles. The election of Matthias was a symbol that the Holy Spirit would not allow betrayal to interfere with the church's progress in establishing the kingdom of God. The invincibility of the Holy Spirit working through the church is a favorite theme of Luke, the author of the Acts. It was a way for him to explain why the world had not yet ended as Jesus and his followers seem to have expected. Members of the church continue Jesus's ministry to bring about the kingdom of God. The Acts of the Apostles describes the Twelve as scattering to the far ends of the earth as missionaries. They were channels of the Spirit's work, participating in and furthering the church's inevitable progress. They disappear from the scene after fulfilling their ministry.

An initial criterion for being called an apostle in the New Testament was having known the historical Jesus, so the Twelve certainly qualified. Membership in this exclusive club expanded pretty early on. Paul never met the historical Jesus but rather the Jesus after his resurrection. He nevertheless calls himself an apostle. As more Gentiles joined the church, the significance of the symbol twelve waned. The Gentiles neither knew nor particularly cared about the reconstitution of the kingdom of

---

[28] Piet Fransen, "Orders and Ordination," *Sacramentum Mundi,* vol. 4 (New York: Herder and Herder, 1969), 307.

Israel. Anyone now could be an apostle. Ministry in the church evolved with changing times, places, and needs.

The New Testament uses the word *diakoneo*, which means "service," to express that which makes a person a disciple of Jesus.[29] Jesus understands himself as one who serves. Luke 12:37 tells the remarkable story of the master who, upon returning home, serves his slaves. In Luke 22:26–27, Jesus reverses the expected pecking order in society again by telling his disciples that those who serve are the greatest among them and that he comes "as one who serves." John's Gospel demonstrates Jesus's understanding of loving service when Jesus washes the disciples' feet and explains that he has given them an example: "You also should do as I have done to you. Very truly I tell you, servants are not greater than their master, nor are messengers greater than the one who sent them" (John 13:1–20). The service that the New Testament has in mind extends to all kinds of different activities that promote the life of the church. It emphasizes that these activities are very practical, as in the story of the last judgment in Matthew 25:31–46. In that story people who feed the hungry, give drink to the thirsty, welcome the stranger, clothe the naked, care for the sick, and visit those in prison are welcomed into heaven; those who have neglected those works are consigned to "the eternal fire prepared for the devil and his angels." Everyday expressions of love are the means for a person to allow grace, the vivifying energy of the Holy Spirit, to make people holy. Neglecting those expressions of love is literally deadly.

The New Testament understands the variety of people's gifts—the catholicity of gifts—as giving life to the church community. Peter's first letter is addressed to a community in distress in the wilds of Asia Minor. The letter encourages the community to understand itself as an integral part of the church, heir to the salvation history told in the Old Testament, and thus "a chosen race, a royal priesthood, a holy nation,

---

[29] Klaus Beyer, "Diakoneo," in *Theological Dictionary of the New Testament*, vol. 2 (Grand Rapids, MI: Eerdmans, 1965), 84–93.

God's own people" who are so chosen "in order that you may proclaim the mighty acts of him who called you out of darkness into his marvelous light" (1 Pet 2:9). The royal priesthood is a participation in Jesus's ministry. Jesus fulfills the priesthood of the Old Testament. They offered, among other things, animal sacrifices that served as vicarious, symbolic offerings of the people themselves to God. Jesus exercises that priesthood by offering not another creature but himself as a sacrifice through all he did, culminating in his self-gift in the Eucharist and on the cross. Later, the letter encourages its readers to exercise that priesthood in practical action: "Like good stewards of the manifold grace of God, serve [a form of *diakoneo*] one another with whatever gift [or charism] each of you has received" (1 Pet 4:10).

Jesus entrusted his priesthood to the church, but, as Piet Fransen states:

> This "idea and reality," to be assimilable, had to be integrated into the social and cultural structures of a given epoch. For the priesthood is a function to be exercised in a human community. Hence it has to accept the functional structures of this community. And this is in fact what took place under the Empire, in the feudal society of the Middle Ages and again later on. The "image" of the priest and the bishop never ceases to evolve.[30]

How people participate in Christ's priesthood, how people exercise ministry, depends on times and places. What works well in one time and place may not work well in another. The important point is that, like everything else in the universe, forms of ministry evolve and adapt to their environment.

New Testament scholar Klaus Beyer writes that the New Testament uses the Greek noun *diakonia* to describe "any 'discharge of service' in genuine love. . . . A decisive point for understanding the concept is that early Christianity learned to

---

[30] Fransen, "Orders and Ordination," 306.

regard and describe as [*diakonia*] all significant activity for the edification of the community (Eph 4:11ff.), a distinction being made according to the mode of operation."[31] In 1 Corinthians 12, Paul elaborates on his understanding of a community in which members get along well—something that the people to whom he was writing were not doing. In an effort to promote communal cooperation he explains to the surly Christians of Corinth:

> There are varieties of gifts [*charisma*], but the same Spirit; and there are varieties of services [*diakonia*], but the same Lord; and there are varieties of activities [*energema*] but it is the same God who activates [*energeo*] all of them in everyone. To each is given the manifestation of the Spirit for the common good. (1 Cor 12:4–7)

All of these services or ministries are energized by the Holy Spirit. They play a role in the life of the body of Christ, which is how Paul describes the church. Ephesians 4 describes the same phenomenon.

A look at the Greek words that Paul uses in 1 Corinthians helps us to appreciate his vision for a variety, that is, a catholicity of ministries. He recognizes the various gifts in the community and that every member of the community has some. Every member is to put those gifts to work: the Greek words *energema* and *energeo* refer to activities in the sense of work and are also related to the Greek word for energy, *energeia*. As scripture scholar Raymond Collins points out, Saint Paul equates ministry with all work that has an eschatological quality to it. In 1 Corinthians 3, Paul describes himself and Apollos as "coworkers" with God, energized by God for the common purpose of building the church, God's temple. Each of them has a specific task based upon his talents in a common, team effort. Paul describes what he does with the same Greek word used for physically constructing a building: *érgon*. Collins writes:

---

[31] Beyer, "Diakoneo," 87.

"By 'work' we should clearly understand 'ministry,' for that is what Paul's [*ergon*] clearly means in this context."[32] What we do, the work in which we engage, will determine the "wages" or "reward" we receive (1 Cor 3:8, 14). Collins interprets this to mean that "the final judgment will be based upon the sort of work that each has done."[33] That is quite an outlook for Paul, the great champion of salvation based on faith rather than on works. The cultivation of our humanity occurs through the activation of the talents or charisms with which God imbues us.

In 1 Corinthians 12:27–28, Paul includes such jobs as teachers, healers, helpers, and administrators among the works in which Christians engage. What Paul is doing is recognizing the value and responsibility of people's collaboration with God in creation. If we free ourselves of the prejudice of the Enlightenment's distinction between the sacred and the secular, we also free ourselves from distinguishing between sacred and secular talents. The image of the church as the body of Christ that Paul offers us beautifully expresses how these talents work. No part of the body is secular and another sacred. First Corinthians 12 and Ephesians 4:12, as well as 1 Peter 4:10, perceive the purpose of the exercise of people's talents as building up the body of Christ. First Corinthians limits itself to speaking of "spiritual matters" (1 Cor 12:1), not because Paul thinks that these are the only charisms but because questions about them were causing problems in the Corinthian community.[34] We mustn't allow his silence here about other talents to give us the impression that he thinks less of them. In addition to using the word *work* to describe his preaching, he also uses it to describe his manual labor (1 Thess 2:9). The Acts of the Apostles identifies this manual labor as that of a cobbler.[35]

---

[32] Raymond F. Collins, "Ministry and the Christian Scriptures," *Louvain Studies* 20 (1995): 117.

[33] Ibid.

[34] Raymond F. Collins, *First Corinthians*, Sacra Pagina 7 (Collegeville, MN: Liturgical Press, 1999), 441–71.

[35] Collins, "Ministry and the Christian Scriptures."

As noted above, in 1 Corinthians 3:9 Paul describes Apollos and himself as God's coworkers *(sunergoi)*, built on the foundation of Christ. In 1 Corinthians 3:5 he describes himself and his coworker, Apollos, as servants: "What then is Apollos? What is Paul? Servants through whom you came to believe, as the Lord assigned to each." The Greek word that Paul uses here is *diakonós*.[36] Elsewhere Paul describes himself as a servant *(diakonós)* of a new covenant (2 Cor 3:6), of God (2 Cor 6:4), and of Christ (2 Cor 11:23). *Diakonía* connotes voluntary work done out of love.[37] It is used approximately one hundred times in the New Testament with meanings ranging from formal offices to government servants—much as *ministry* is used today. Jesus himself is described as a *diakonós* in Romans 15:8 and as one who serves *(diakoneo)* in Mark 10:45, Matthew 10:26, and Luke 22:27. Paul thinks of this collaboration with God as extremely important. He even sees a relation between our collaboration with God and the final judgment; what the world will look like in the future really depends upon what we do with it. God's contribution is assured. God provides the guidance and the energy. The incarnate Son is the way to salvation and fulfillment, and the Holy Spirit is the energy and counselor. All we have to do is cooperate.

Paul's identification of his ministry as work and his understanding of that work as one of service are clear. Can we invert the assertion? If Paul's ministry is work and service, are his work and service ministry? Was Paul's manual labor a ministry? Since Paul's manual labor was an expression of a God-given talent, that is, since his manual labor flowed from one of his charisms for the service of the good of the community, it certainly appears that we can label it ministry. If the goal of all ministry is the building up of the church as the body of Christ,[38] does it not follow that all work that builds up the body of Christ is ministry? Ministry is work because

---

[36] Ibid., 121.
[37] Collins, *First Corinthians*, 153.
[38] Ibid.

it is an expression of people's charisms. It follows that work that is the expression of people's charisms is ministry. It is not necessary that people expressing their charisms in work think of it as ministry. They don't have to be conscious that their work is a collaboration with God's creative activity in order for it actually to *be* a collaboration with God's creative activity. How many people promote the realization of the kingdom of God without reflecting on it in such a way? They may be Christians, non-Christians, or atheists who just go about their work as an expression of their love for humankind. They may be manual laborers or professionals. It suffices that the work be done by people who follow their consciences, judging that their work is a service to the community at large, for us to think of it as ministry. It is, however, important also to specify that not all work is ministry. People work at all kinds of jobs that are abuses of charisms. The work of people who violate or ignore their consciences is not ministry. Such work is not motivated by the desire to put charisms into action for the upbuilding of the kingdom of God.

The Synoptic tradition, that is, the Gospels of Matthew, Mark, and Luke, understands Jesus as the "Suffering Servant" referred to in the Book of Isaiah (42:1–4; 49:1–6; 50:4–9; 52:13—53:12). The innocent suffering of this mysterious figure in Isaiah was thought to bring salvation to a sinful people. Jesus's service first finds expression in miracles, signaling the coming of the kingdom of God, and then the fullness of salvation through the cross and resurrection. It is important to remember that service as understood in the New Testament did not distinguish between spiritual and physical needs. "Service is meant to cater to the whole person," as illustrated in the story of the Last Judgment in Matthew 25:31–46.[39] People are expected to be of service to others in their physical needs. Jesus's disciples participate in and continue his service. Like Jesus they are expected to empty themselves, taking the form of a slave

---

[39] A. W. Swamidoss, "Diakonia as Servanthood in the Synoptics," *The Indian Journal of Theology* 32 (1983): 37.

(Phil 2:7).[40] The service to the community serves to attract people to empty themselves of selfishness and self-centeredness in order to participate in the community that is the church.[41]

Another word in the New Testament that has the connotation of service is *doulos*, that is, *slave*. The ancient usage of the term is curiously linked to that of *diakonós*. It always connotes absolute submission but does not necessarily imply humiliation. Being the slave of a high-ranking person could even be an honor.[42] The idea is carried over from the Old Testament, in which the Israelites thought of their relationship with God as one between slave and master. This relationship implied that the Israelites recognized their absolute dependence on God, their creator and source of all life. It carried along with it the consecration of all their activities to God.[43] All their work was thus an expression of their relationship with God.

The New Testament expands on the theme of how slaves collaborate with God in promoting the coming of his reign. Luke offers Mary as a paradigm for Christians when she declares herself the "slave of the Lord." Her submission to God is the means for the incarnation, the fullness of the presence of the Son in creation (Luke 1:38). Her subsequent canticle (Luke 1:46–55) expresses to Elizabeth her joy at having been chosen to collaborate with God to fulfill the promises of the Old Testament. Paul offers his own body as a slave (1 Cor 9:27). Philippians 2:6–11 identifies the Son himself as taking on the form of a slave. He attributes the assumption of such a state to *kenosis*, the emptying of self out of love that characterizes each member of the Holy Trinity. Denis Edwards, a

---

[40] Ibid.

[41] Johannes Ries and H. J. Hendriks, "Koinonia en diakonia as 'n missionale koninkryksdans," *HTS Teologiese Studies/Theological Studies* 69–2 (2013): art. #1249.

[42] C. Spicq, "Le Vocabulaire de l'Esclavage dans le Nouveau Testament," *Revue Biblique* 85 (1978): 208.

[43] Ibid., 210. "qu'ils sont tenus de consacrer toute leur activité au service de leur *Kyrios*."

theologian with a great interest in evolution, reflects upon creation and redemption as taking place within the great kenotic dynamic of the three persons of the Trinity.[44] We humans become ever more human through the process of deification, that is, the more we become part of God. All that we do that is authentically human is an expression of the altruistic love that is God. The Letter to the Colossians instructs slaves to work for their human masters "from the soul," that is, wholeheartedly, knowing that their reward will come from the Lord (Col 3:22–24). The letter considers their work a collaboration with salvation history.

Kenosis makes room for the Holy Spirit. That is true for the Father and the Son, and it is true for us. People who empty themselves, taking on the form of a slave, participate in the divine act of love. They breathe in the Holy Spirit thanks to their kenosis. The very act of emptying the self allows the Holy Spirit to transform people from slaves to children of God (Gal 4:7; Rom 8:15–17; Philem 16).

The Bible understands ministry as the immanent activity of people inspired by the Holy Spirit, the divine, transcendent energy, who works through people's work to bring people into greater communion. This activity is a continuation of the Holy Spirit's activity that we first perceive in the Big Bang. The Spirit energizes matter to form increasingly complex open systems, one of which we call the church. The Spirit inspires all members to activate the gifts with which God endows them through nature and to use them to promote the convergence of the universe, to use one of Teilhard's favorite images. Meinert Grumm sums up the idea: "The essence of ministry, given to all (1 Cor 12:4–6; Eph 4:11–12), is to exercise our gifts of service in the body of Christ toward his ends. Both worship and ministry are subsumed under the common term 'serve/service.'"[45]

---

[44] Denis Edwards, *The God of Evolution: A Trinitarian Theology* (Mahwah, NJ: Paulist Press, 1999), 31.

[45] Grumm, "Ministry," 107.

Ordination in the New Testament?

The question of whether anyone in the New Testament was ordained is a tricky one. The term *ordination* has taken on different meanings during the church's lifetime. There was no such thing as ordination in the New Testament as we understand the term today. Today we think of incorporation into what the Vatican II document *Lumen gentium* refers to as a group of people whose ministry is essentially different (*LG* 44). *Essence* is a term from Greek metaphysical philosophy. It refers to an aspect of something that actually defines what it is. The council thinks that the ministry of people who are ordained and those who are not is profoundly, essentially, different, though interrelated. Such a distinction is not found in the New Testament, and it appears that the writers of the New Testament did not see any need for it. Theologian P. De Clerck understands any rites that look like what people today would think of as ordination as really a social investiture to acknowledge and demonstrate divine investiture into a ministry. He quotes J. Delorme:

> In all cases [of investiture], the charism constitutes the competence of the servant: it qualifies him and makes him apt to serve. . . . It may simply be a question of a charism that the community recognizes. . . . When there is ordination by the imposition of hands, the need for competence received from God is not diminished, but doubly affirmed: before putting someone in charge, one questions him concerning his aptitude to fulfill his task and, in conferring the charge, prayer, fasting and the act of the imposition of hands asks for and signifies the gift of the Spirit.[46]

---

[46] J. Delorme et al., *Le ministère et les ministères selon le Nouveau Testament*, coll. Parole de Dieu 10 (Paris: Éditions du Seuil, 1974). Quoted in P. De Clerck, "Ordination, Ordre," *Catholicisme Hier-Aujourd'hui-Demain* (Paris: Letouzey et Ané vol. X, 1985), col. 162–206.

It is only in the second century, with the Latin African writer Tertullian, that the word *order* appears with reference to a group of ministers. The ritual of laying on of hands that we find in the New Testament, as in 1 Timothy 5:22, signified that the person was chosen by God and the people to fulfill a specific ministry in the community.

The laying on of hands was not associated with priestly ordination in Judaism. Numbers 8:5–11 does describe a rite of laying on of hands of the Tribe of Levi, who exercised priestly functions in Israel, but this was not an ordination rite. Rather, it signified the members of the tribe as sin offerings for the people. Fortunately for the Levites, after the people laid hands on them, they laid hands on bulls, who were sacrificed in place of the Levites. At other times people laid hands on other people as a symbol, a kind of sacrament, of blessing and transferal of power. In the New Testament the laying on of hands signified the handing on of mission. It was not an ordination. In fact, the rite of ordination as we know it probably developed about 200 CE. Piet Fransen concludes, "It may therefore be presumed that the laying on of hands is not a 'substantial' element of the sacramental rite, but a rite instituted by the church."[47]

So, was anyone ordained in the New Testament? No, not if we use the understanding of ordination from *Lumen gentium*. Does that mean that the church does not have the right to ordain people? Again, no. Catholicism considers the Bible as a vehicle of God's self-revelation, helping us to know God more and more, relate to him, and respond to his call to salvation. It is normative for theology in the sense that it serves as a guide or a canon for us to understand our faith in different times and circumstances. We are not, however, stuck in the culture of the first century. Catholicism also looks to the church's tradition for revelation. The Vatican II document *Dei verbum (On Divine Revelation)*, gives a clear definition of what Catholicism understands by its tradition:

---

[47] Fransen, "Orders and Ordination," 311.

Now what was handed on by the Apostles includes everything which contributes toward the holiness of life and increase in faith of the peoples of God; and so the church, in her teaching, life and worship, perpetuates and hands on to all generations all that she herself is, all that she believes.

This tradition which comes from the Apostles develop[s] in the Church with the help of the Holy Spirit. For there is a growth in the understanding of the realities and the words which have been handed down. This happens through the contemplation and study made by believers, who treasure these things in their hearts (see Luke, 2:19, 51) through a penetrating understanding of the spiritual realities which they experience, and through the preaching of those who have received through Episcopal succession the sure gift of truth. For as the centuries succeed one another, the Church constantly moves forward toward the fullness of divine truth until the words of God reach their complete fulfillment in her. (*DV* 8)

The council recognizes that the God who reveals himself is always the same, but our understanding of him and of how to relate to him evolves along with everything else in creation. As Vatican II's document on ecumenism states: "Christ summons the Church to continual reformation as she sojourns here on earth" (*Unitatis redintegratio* 6).[48] Pope Francis in his *Apostolic Constitution "Veritatis gaudium" on Ecclesiastical Universities and Faculties* encourages theologians to find new ways of expressing the same Christian faith in different cultural contexts:

In the diversity of peoples who experience the gift of God, each in accordance with its own culture, the Church expresses her genuine catholicity and shows forth "the beauty of her varied face." In the Christian customs of an

---

[48] See further ibid., 99ff.

evangelized people, the Holy Spirit adorns the Church, showing her new aspects of revelation and giving her a new face. . . .

With a fine image, Benedict XVI stated that the Church's tradition "is not transmission of things or of words, a collection of dead things. Tradition is the living river that links us to the origins, the living river in which the origins are ever present. This river irrigates various lands, feeds various geographical places, germinating the best of that land, the best of that culture. In this way, the Gospel continues to be incarnated in every corner of the world, in an ever new Way." (4d)

It is our task to figure out how to incarnate the gospel in ways that are meaningful to people in the twenty-first century. The forms of ministry need not be identical throughout the world in a church that is catholic. The forms of ministry must help different people engage in and contribute to the life of the church evolving toward heaven.

The Catholic Church's understanding of the role of tradition corresponds to the evolutionary concept of biocultural evolution. In terms of the evolutionary cosmology that we have been talking about in this book, the church is an open system of matter that processes energy just like all other open systems that scientists describe in the universe. It is a social structure organized by people in such a way as to maximize our success in natural selection. From the theological perspective, success means participation in the community of God. We achieve success by listening to the Word spoken by the Father that summons us to develop into that community by the power of the Holy Spirit. That Word and that Spirit are alive; better yet, they *are* life! We are not frozen in time, obligated to live the lifestyles and social structures envisioned in the Bible. That is a fundamentalist interpretation of scripture. We are not people of the Book; we are the people of God, who is dynamic. The *perichoresis*, the dynamic and evolving relationships among the persons of the Holy Trinity, characterizes

salvation history.[49] The same dynamic and evolving relationships also characterize the church and the activities in which
its members engage. They have changed and evolved in the
past, and there is no reason why they cannot continue to
change and evolve in the future. The scientific perspective
supports this theological insight. In the next chapter we will
take a closer look at what biocultural evolution is and how
it works in the church's tradition in formulating theologies
of ministry after the New Testament.

---

[49] See Edwards, *The God of Evolution*.

Chapter 3

Ministry in the Church's Tradition

The first part of Pierre Teilhard de Chardin's mystical meditation on creation, *The Divine Milieu*, is a reflection on the value of human work in creation's evolution. He calls this part of his book "the divinization of our activities." We humans participate in the birth of the universe as Paul imagines the process in Romans 8. Teilhard muses: "Each one of our works, by its more or less remote or direct effect upon the spiritual world, helps to make perfect Christ in his mystical totality."[1] He continues:

> Our work appears to us, in the main, as a way of earning our daily bread. But its essential virtue is on a higher level: through it we complete in ourselves the subject of the divine union; and through it again we somehow make to grow in stature the divine term of the one with whom we are united, our Lord Jesus Christ.[2]

All of human work, insists Teilhard, has the potential to advance the evolution of creation to its ultimate goal. He rejects a dichotomy of sacred and profane: "By virtue of the Creation

---

[1] Pierre Teilhard de Chardin, *The Divine Milieu* (New York: Harper Torchbooks, 1965), 62.

[2] Ibid., 63.

and, still more, of the Incarnation, nothing here below is *profane* for those who know how to see."[3]

Teilhard recognizes that we human beings, and the work we do, lie on a continuum of work that we can trace back to the Big Bang, the beginning of creation as we know it. Teilhard traces this continuum from its genesis through humanity in *The Human Phenomenon*. He looks at evolution through the eyes of a scientist as it progresses through time. He explains, with considerable enthusiasm, how matter—stuff—becomes more and more complex, and he really gets excited as he identifies the evolution of consciousness in humanity. Human consciousness provides all kinds of evolutionary advantages—otherwise it would not have lasted. Remember, natural selection favors characteristics that provide some advantage for survival in a competitive and selfish world. Humans are not the only creatures that exhibit consciousness, but we do seem to bring it to new heights. Dogs, for example, are conscious and engage in activity that cultivates canine survival. They communicate with one another and, perhaps even more to their advantage, they've learned to communicate with us. They cooperate, learn, and engage in activities that promote their welfare. Their consciousness, however, appears to be limited to the immanent dimension of reality.

Human consciousness does all that canine consciousness does plus provides us the ability to know the transcendent dimension of reality. We observe the increasing complexity of matter under the influence of energy in evolution, and we wonder if it has meaning. We, as far as I can tell, are the only animals that ask *why* things happen. We want to know if this whole evolutionary thing is going anywhere. What's it all about? Is there a meaningful end to all this cosmic activity?

Part of the development of human consciousness is human conscience. As we saw in Chapter 1, the two words sound suspiciously alike, and have the same root meaning "to know

---

[3] Ibid., 66.

with," "share knowledge with another," or "be aware." In 1 Corinthians 8:7, Saint Paul takes his readers in Corinth to task for apparently being unaware of "this knowledge," which is that "there is one God, the Father, from whom all things and for whom we exist, and one Lord, Jesus Christ, through whom are all things and through whom we exist." There you have it. Why do we exist? For God. First Peter 2:19 credits our awareness of God as that which gives us the courage to endure anything. Hebrews 10:2 describes our ability to be conscious of sin. Acts 23:1 and 1 Timothy 3:9 refer to "clear consciences." All these texts use the same word in Greek: *suneidesis*.

The development of human consciousness and conscience must have some evolutionary advantage. Teilhard sees the evolutionary advantage of consciousness and conscience as promoting our evolution toward the reason for our existence: participation in the community of God. He muses on the significance of this development from the standpoint of Christian faith in the epilogue to *The Human Phenomenon*. Here he recognizes that biological evolution in humans has "reached a ceiling." The way forward is human socialization.[4]

Biocultural Evolution and the Church's Tradition

The relatively new field of biocultural evolution seems to be the answer to Teilhard's vision for humanity's way forward in evolution. Scholars in the 1960s began to look seriously at what people do with all the consciousness, awareness, and conscience that has developed through biological evolution. What we do is engage in activities that cultivate us. We engage

---

[4] Pierre Teilhard de Chardin, *The Human Phenomenon*, trans. Sarah Appleton Weber (Portland, OR: Sussex Academic Press, 1999), 220. Originally published in French as *Le phénomène humain* (Paris: Éditions du Seuil, 1955).

in human culture. Culture is actually a development of evolution. It develops because it offers some advantage in natural selection. Culture is what complex things, which we often refer to as living, do to promote their chances of survival. All creatures engage in culture in one form or another. As the old song says, though in a different context, "birds do it, bees do it, even educated fleas do it." Beavers, for example, use their consciousness to cultivate themselves by building dams to create cozy pools in which to build nests. By nature and nurture they know how to build those dams that ensure their own individual safety and give their offspring a better chance at growing up—to do the same thing. They know the immanent dimension of reality. That is beaver culture.

Human culture appears to be the most sophisticated on earth. People all over the world engage in all kinds of activities that shape who individuals become, who groups of persons become, and what the whole planet becomes. We engage with our environment and use our talents inherited from physical evolution to promote our survival. In so doing we, like beavers, influence our environment. And why stop with earth? Now that people are capable of interplanetary travel, we are engaging with and influencing what happens beyond our own planetary home. As far as we know, however, beavers don't ask themselves questions like why they build dams, why they want their offspring to grow up, or the effects that their dams have on the environment. Many people, alas, don't ask those questions either, but we *can*. And that very ability puts us in a different category from beavers or any other animals.

Human consciousness is capable of having some knowledge of the transcendent dimension of reality as well as the immanent. Human culture adds meaning, responsibility, a much higher degree of innovation, and the possibility of a transcendent goal to beaver culture. Human culture is so rich that language evolved to ensure, among other things, that it passes from one generation to the next through cooperative action.[5] Human culture takes various forms in different parts of the world depending on the local environment, but human culture itself is universal among humans. We all engage in promoting our evolution through work. What work we do is a result of biological evolution and instinct but also of the conscious choices that result from the use of our conscience. What we do is inspired by what we think are the source and goal of life, the meaning of life, the answer to why we build not only dams but farms, cities, bridges, churches; why we want our children to grow up, and, hopefully, the effects of what we do on the environment.

Insofar as human culture is focused on God as its ultimate goal, and its work is inspired by God, we can speak of what Catholic theology calls the church's Tradition. The church's Tradition is what people do as a result of their consciousness of the God who is the source and goal of life and who reveals life's meaning. Christian culture understands itself as a culture that continues to evolve from the Big Bang and, more specifically through the history of Israel, the event of Jesus Christ, and the history of the Christian community. It looks at creation through the lens of the fullness of the revelation of God, Jesus. It works in and through creation, the immanent dimension of reality, conscious of God as revealed through Jesus, the transcendent dimension of reality. God is Christian culture's source, inspiration, and goal. The church's Tradition is the theological version of biocultural evolution.[6]

Scientists who study biocultural evolution recognize that among the patterns of behavior that we humans develop and

---

[5] See Terrence W. Deacon, "Why a Brain Capable of Language Evolved Only Once: Prefrontal Cortex and Symbolic Learning," *Zygon* 31 (1996): 635–69; idem, *The Symbolic Species: The Co-Evolution of Language and the Brain* (London: W. W. Norton, 1997); Steven Pinker, *The Language Instinct* (New York: William Morrow, 1994).

[6] See Philip Hefner, *The Human Factor: Evolution, Culture, and Religion* (Minneapolis: Fortress Press, 1993), 19.

engage in are competition and cooperation. They are our evolutionary inheritance. As far back in evolution as we can peer
we see these two behaviors at work.[7] One of the manifestations
of the eusociality that characterizes us is working together for
a common good. Few things get us going as much as a common enemy—one of the reasons we like competitive sports so
much. But that instinct to work together can be directed to
noncompetitive activities as well, as in the challenge to get a
job done that will benefit one another, either immediately or in
the future. Social scientists tell us that we sometimes cooperate and help one another out so others will help us when we
need it. There is always at least a grain of selfishness, of sin,
in our motivations for helping others, in cooperating for the
common good.[8] Nature has developed in such a way that at
some subconscious level we all ask, What's in it for me? This is

---

[7] See Martin A. Nowak and Roger Highfield, *SuperCooperators:
Altruism, Evolution and Why We Need Each Other to Succeed* (New
York: Free Press, 2011); Patrick Bateson, "Co-operation," *Theology* 89
(1986): 5–10; Claudia Canegallo, Guido Ortona, Stefania Ottone, Fer-
ruccio Ponzano, Francesco Scacciati, "Competition versus Cooperation: Some Experimental Evidence," *The Journal of Socio-Economics*
37 (2008): 18–30; Robert Axelrod, *The Evolution of Cooperation*
(Cambridge, MA: Basic Books, 2006); Samuel Bowles and Herbert
Gintis, *A Cooperative Species: Human Reciprocity and Its Evolution*
(Princeton, NJ: Princeton University Press, 2011); Martin A. Nowak
and Natalia L. Komarova, "The Evolution of Altruism: From Game
Theory to Human Language," *Spiritual Information: 100 Perspec-
tives on Science and Religion*, ed. Charles L. Harper, Jr. (Philadelphia:
Templeton Foundation Press, 2005): 308–14; Martin Nowak, *Evolu-
tionary Dynamics: Exploring the Equations of Life* (Cambridge, MA:
Harvard University Press, 2006); David Rand and Martin Nowak,
"Human Cooperation," *Trends in Cognitive Sciences* 17 (2013):
413–25; Matt Ridley, *The Origins of Virtue: Human Instincts and
the Evolution of Cooperation* (New York: Penguin, 1997); Michael
Tomasello, *Why We Cooperate* (Cambridge, MA: A Boston Review
Book, 2009); E. O. Wilson, *The Social Conquest of Earth* (New York:
Liveright Publishing Corporation, 2012). Cf. Stephen J. Pope, "E. O.
Wilson as Moralist," *Zygon* 36 (2001): 233–40.
[8] See Anders Nygren, *Agape and Eros*, trans. Philip S. Watson
(New York: Harper and Row, 1969).

what we traditionally have called original sin. Salvation history is the process by which God liberates us from the selfishness with which evolution has bequeathed us. It culminates in the death and resurrection of Christ, in whom we die to sin and are reborn in the community of the Trinity, in which there is no trace of selfishness, in which the persons love and work together in absolute altruism.[9] Christians join Christ in this process through Christian sacramental initiation. One of the effects of that sacramental initiation is to give us the grace to work cooperatively to build up the body of Christ.

The Tradition of the Catholic Church is the story of people doing their best to respond to the grace of Christian initiation. It is the story of how human culture under the influence of grace abandons sin and is deified.[10] In the words of theologian Philip Hefner, people are "created co-creators" with God.[11] By engaging in culture, we play a crucial role in the direction and form that evolution takes, for better or for worse. When human culture is inspired by a combination of selfishness and altruism, it is doomed to a Sisyphean future. Just as Sisyphus was condemned forever to roll a rock up a hill only to see it roll back down before he got to the top, human culture without transformative grace will never break the endless cycle of the formation of cooperative groups marked by altruism and their breakdown due to

---

[9] See further Daryl P. Domning and Monika K. Hellwig, *Original Selfishness* (Burlington, VT: Ashgate, 2006); Donald C. Maldari, SJ, "The Evolution of the Messianic Age: The Metamorphosis from Competitive Selfishness to Selfless, Altruistic, Cooperative Love," *Louvain Studies* 36 (2012): 372–96.

[10] See Ralph Wendell Burhoe, "Religion's Role in Human Evolution: The Missing Link between Ape-Man's Selfish Genes and Civilized Altruism," *Zygon* 14 (1979): 135–62; Philip Hefner, "The Spiritual Task of Religion in Culture: An Evolutionary Perspective," *Zygon* 33 (1998): 535–44; idem, "The Animal That Aspires to Be an Angel: The Challenge of Transhumanism," *Dialog: A Journal of Theology* 48 (2009): 158–67.

[11] Philip Hefner, *The Human Factor: Evolution, Culture, and Religion* (Minneapolis: Augsburg Fortress, 1993).

selfishness.[12] We all need to die to selfishness, to sin, with Christ, and to rise, to be reborn with him in the fullness of creation.

The Catholicity of the Church's Tradition

In 381 CE the second ecumenical council met in the city of Constantinople, the imperial capital. The main reason for the council was to deal with the question of the divinity of the Holy Spirit. It took centuries for Christian theologians to work out some understanding of the Holy Trinity. Christians reflected upon their experiences of God, especially as expressed by first-century biblical writers, and came to the unwieldy conclusion that God is one and three at the same time. It's quite understandable that some people had trouble grasping how one equals three. Monotheism was, and is, essential to the Christian faith, as well as to that of Judaism and Islam. There are not two or three gods: only one. The Book of Deuteronomy proclaims it and exhorts Jews literally to remember it several times a day: "Hear, O Israel, the LORD is our God, the LORD alone." Christians all agreed that what they called the Father was God, but what about the Son and the Holy Spirit?

In 325 CE the Council of Nicaea discussed the character of the Son in light of the proposal by a man named Arius that the Son, though extraordinary, was a creature, not divine. The archbishop of Alexandria in Egypt, Athanasius, essentially argued that a creature was incapable of saving the world. A creature, however extraordinary, was part of creation and could not bring creation beyond its sinfulness. Only God could do that, so the Son had to be divine if he was to save us. The Council of Nicaea eventually agreed with Athanasius and proclaimed the creed of Nicaea. This declared that Christians believe that the Son, through whom the Father creates, is divine and of the same being as the Father. Nevertheless, Arius's position took centuries to die out.

---

[12] Nowak and Highfield, *SuperCooperators.* Cf. Wilson, *The Social Conquest of Earth,* 297.

Shortly after the Council of Nicaea the same question came up regarding the divinity of the Holy Spirit. The same arguments were put forward, and the Council of Constantinople came to the same conclusion. The council issued the creed of Constantinople, which elaborates on the third article of the Christian faith: belief in the Holy Spirit. This creed continued to use the language that the creed of Nicaea used regarding the divinity of the Son but avoided calling the Holy Spirit one in being with the Father because of all the theological "feathers" that expression had ruffled a few decades earlier. It made it clear that Christians believe that the Holy Spirit is divine and went on to describe the church in the same paragraph. The church, the body of Christ, is animated by the Holy Spirit; that is, the Holy Spirit is the divine energy that brings people together and counsels us on how to live. They described the church as one, holy, catholic, and apostolic.

The Catholicity of the Church

What exactly the Council of Constantinople meant by "catholic" is, alas, not immediately obvious. The word *catholic* itself is a Greek adjective. It is a combination of two other Greek words: *katá* and *hólos*. *Katá* is a preposition; the meanings of prepositions in any language are very slippery. Anyone who has tried to learn a foreign language knows that the rules for prepositions are made to be broken. The preposition *katá* is, unfortunately, no exception. It can mean any of the following: "downwards," "distributively of a whole divided into parts," "toward," "according to," "throughout or among," or "in the manner of."[13] *Hólos*, a noun, is easier to translate; it basically means "whole, entire" or even "the universe."[14] In classical

---

[13] For standard references in the field, see Henry George Liddell and Robert Scott, *A Greek-English Lexicon* and *An Intermediate Greek-English Lexicon*; William J. Slater, *Lexicon to Pindar*.

[14] Liddell and Scott, *A Greek-English Lexicon*.

Greek *katholikós* meant "general," as in the expression *in general* or *universal*.[15]

Patristics scholar J.N.D. Kelly explains that for ancient Christians such as those who composed the creed of Constantinople, *katholikós* had the sense of *general* as opposed to *specific* or *individual*. He notes, however, that Christian usage of the word tended to convey a sense of "single or unique, inasmuch as whatever is truly universal is in that respect one."[16] In other words, if I say that in general people like ice cream, that means that lots of *different* people enjoy eating ice cream. There is diversity in unity—lots of different people—and unity in diversity—they like the same thing.

The first Christian text to use the word *catholic* to describe the church was from Saint Ignatius of Antioch in the middle of the second century CE. Ignatius writes:

> Let that be reckoned as valid Eucharist which is celebrated under the bishop or someone commissioned by him; for wherever the bishop appears, there is the community *(plethos)*, just as wherever Christ Jesus is; there is the catholic church *(he katholike ekklesia)*.[17]

Wolfgang Beinert, a professor of theology at the University of Regensburg, thinks that Ignatius's understanding of the church's catholicity flowed out of his Christology, that is, how he understood who Christ was.[18] Ignatius developed his understanding of who Christ was and what his role is

---

[15] Ibid.

[16] J.N.D. Kelly, "'Catholic' and 'Apostolic' in the Early Centuries," *One in Christ* 6 (1970): 275. See further Vittorino Grossi, "Nota sobre la semántica de la expresión 'Iglesia católica' antes y después del 'Edicto' de Constantino del 313," *Anuario de Historia de la Iglesia* 22 (2013): 111–33.

[17] Ignatius of Antioch, *Ad Smyrnaeos* 8.2, in *The Apostolic Fathers*, ed. J. B. Lightfoot (New York: Macmillan, 1891), 158. Quoted in Kelly, "'Catholic' and 'Apostolic' in the Early Centuries," 276.

[18] Wolfgang Beinert, "Catholicity as a Property of the Church," *The Jurist* 52 (1992): 456.

in salvation history through controversy with the Gnostics. Gnostics focused on knowledge as a means of salvation. Their basic intuition was good and shared by orthodox Christians. The Christians understood knowledge as intimate connection with God. It's something like what we mean when we say we know a friend well. It's a relationship that is not superficial but very deep and personal. That kind of relationship with God is the goal of salvation history. Knowledge is not something physical, even if it occurs using physical means. For example, we need a physical brain to know something, but dissecting a brain to find out what someone knows will have a frustrating result for all concerned. The Gnostics denigrated anything physical, finding it not so much the means of knowing but a limitation to knowing. The body insists on things like eating, sleeping, healthcare, and so on, which take time and attention away from knowing. They thought of that which was physical as corrupt. They understood knowing as spiritual, and so they valued that which was spiritual. Gnostics denied that the Son of God would become flesh, because flesh was physical and therefore corrupt. For them, the Son came to take humanity out of the flesh.

In contrast with the Gnostics, Ignatius emphasized the real incarnation, that is, the enfleshment, the physical reality of the Son of God in the person of Jesus. He saw Christ bringing all of creation, including all sinful flesh, together into union with God. The Son became incarnate, according to Ignatius, in order to save the flesh, not to discard it. Bishops were, for Ignatius, symbols of Christ. Christ, through the work of bishops, gathered disparate peoples together into a "catholic" church. Ignatius's understanding of church as the *ekklesía* was twofold. On the one hand, there were individual church communities united by their individual bishops. On the other, there was the worldwide *ekklesía*, that is, the general church to which the individual churches belong.

In the fourth century Cyril of Jerusalem explained his understanding of the church's catholicity as the quality of being found everywhere. The church is catholic because it includes all kinds of people, teaches everything that anyone needs to know for salvation, heals sin, and imparts virtue.[19] His description sounds a lot like that of the Holy Trinity. The "catholic" church draws all people from all cultures into unity without violating their individuality. It continues to speak the word in such a way that everyone can understand. It heals divisions and provides the strength to work with God as co-creators of the world.

In time *catholic* came to distinguish the true church from the heretical ones. It did so because universality was an indication of the church's authenticity.[20] This universality was never equated with uniformity. Universality meant, and still means, unity.

Belgian theologian Gustav Thils devoted his life's work to studying the catholicity of the church and its implications. He was a *peritus* or theological adviser to the bishops at Vatican II and worked for years in the ecumenical movement. He offers particularly rich insights into the meaning of *catholicity* in Christian theology today. Thils notes that *catholicity* can be thought of in both quantitative terms, such as place, number, and time, and in qualitative terms, such as the transcendence of particularities and adaptation to everything. The quantitative mindset predominated especially after the Reformation in the sixteenth century, but that shifted to the qualitative understanding in the twentieth century.[21] In the quantitative understanding of catholicity the church is catholic because it is expanding to include everybody in the world. In the qualitative understanding the church is catholic because it embraces different ways of living the Christian faith.

Thinking of the catholicity of the church in qualitative terms invites us to look upon the data and theories of the universe's evolution through the eyes of faith. We see that the ancient

---

[19] Cyril of Jerusalem, *Catecheses*, 18:23, *Patrologia Graeca* [hereafter PG], 33: 1047. Cited in Avery Dulles, SJ, *The Catholicity of the Church* (Oxford: Clarendon Press, 1985), 14.

[20] Kelly, "'Catholic' and 'Apostolic' in the Early Centuries," 278–79.

[21] Gustav Thils, "La Notion de catholicité de l'église à l'époque moderne," *Ephemerides theologicae Lovanienses* 13 (1936): 5–7.

church's understanding of its catholicity sounds remarkably similar to how physics understands the universe. That's not by accident. The church operates according to the same principles as everything in the universe because the church exists in the universe. Physics studies the universe from the viewpoint of reason alone. It studies the immanent dimension of reality. Theology studies the universe from the viewpoint of faith in dialog with reason. It studies the transcendent dimension of reality.

The universe is catholic in a way similar to how Ignatius and Cyril thought of the church as catholic. The universe consists of individual and diverse open systems—neutrons, protons, atoms, molecules, right up to galaxies—that all work together in a transcendent, synergistic whole. Avery Dulles writes:

> In the widest sense of the term, catholicity may be predicated of the universe as a whole. The entire cosmos has in Christ its centre of unity, coherence, and fulfilment (cf. Col 1:17). Nature is essentially good and perfectible; it is, as Bonhoeffer said, "directed to the coming of Christ," who is at work recapitulating the cosmos under his universal headship (cf. Eph 1:10).[22]

The church, too, consists of individual and diverse communities that all work together in a transcendent, synergistic whole. Just as every particle in the universe contributes something to its own open system and to the whole universe, so every member of the church contributes to the life of his or her own local community and to the universal church around the world. Because catholicity is a pattern of nature it is part of what has traditionally been called the natural law. The natural law comprises the patterns that faith perceives in nature that reveal God's will.[23] It follows, therefore, that ministry, what people

---

[22] Dulles, *The Catholicity of the Church*, 168.

[23] See further Josef Fuchs, SJ, *Natural Law: A Theological Investigation*, trans. Helmut Reckter, SJ, and John A. Bowlin (New York: Sheed and Ward, 1965); Mark Graham, *Josef Fuchs on Natural Law* (Washington, DC: Georgetown University Press, 2002).

in the church do for the life of the church community, must be catholic if it is to be authentic.

Through the eyes of faith we see the why and wherefore of the natural processes created by God and of human work as participating in these processes. With Teilhard we see plurality, unity, and energy at work in the matter of the universe that is permeated by the body of Christ. We see the foreshadowing of the church "from the beginning of the world," as the Vatican II document *Lumen gentium* claims (*LG* 2).[24] The evolution of humanity marks a new epoch in this evolutionary saga. It is through the church that God brings all creation into convergence, into community, ultimately into communion with God, the Holy Trinity.

The Development of Ministry in the First Century

The church's Tradition is generally understood to be the story of the way people continue the work of salvation that the writers of the Bible so powerfully and beautifully expressed. Like the stories in the Bible, the Tradition is the story of people responding, or not responding, to God's call—God's vocation—to bring creation to fulfillment. The Bible is checkered with stories of how people say yes, no, and maybe to God. Only a few are presented as giving an unequivocal yes, and most of those are women: Naomi, Ruth, Rahab, Susanna in the Old Testament, and just about all the women in the New Testament, starting with Mary. Those giving an unequivocal no are exemplars of selfishness. Among this hit parade are Egypt's unnamed pharaoh during the Exodus, Jezebel, Nebuchadnezzar, and Herod the Great. Most of the time, however, people in the Bible give a maybe. They're filled with the best of intentions but life gets

---

[24] See also Thomas Aquinas, *The Aquinas Catechism: A Simple Explanation of the Catholic Faith by the Church's Greatest Theologian*, article 9 (Manchester, NH: Sophia Institute Press, 2000), 81. *In symbolum Apostolorum, Opusculum VII* (Parma ed.), vol. xvi, pp. 135–51, art. IX, p. 148—traces the church back to Abel.

in the way. Abraham, Isaac, Jacob, Moses, and Samson stand out in the Old Testament; in the New Testament all of Jesus's disciples with the exception of the women abandon him, led by Peter.

The church's Tradition, true to its name, continues this pattern of varying responses to God. And it does so with the same starts, stops, and hiccups we find in the Bible. The history of the Catholic Church alone has made for a lot of good movies, complete with saints, villains, and everything in between. The development of ministry within the church's Tradition bears the marks of the people who participate in the great drama of salvation history. Some of that development has been a brilliant success, some a dreadful failure, and most a mixture of the two.

Paul's image of Jesus's disciples as the body of Christ does an excellent job of describing the dynamics of the Christian community after the resurrection. Paul expresses the sense that has become pervasive in Christianity that through baptism we die to sin through Christ and are raised with him "so that we too might walk in newness of life" (Rom 6:3). Free of sin, we no longer live for ourselves but "to God" because it is Christ who lives in us (Gal 2:19–20). The expression "to God" is rich in meaning. It describes a deep personal relationship (see also Col 2:20).[25] The activities of the body of Christ are described in the letters to the Corinthians, Ephesians, and Colossians: all members of the community have charisms, talents, gifts from God that they exercise in love through their various ministries. This exercise benefits both the life and growth of the community as well as the persons exercising them. The expression of love—the "pressing out" of love, as the word *express* indicates—is precisely the way people live and grow into their true selves, the image of God. Important here is to recognize that all members of the community have the opportunity to express this love, that is, to exercise their ministries.

---

[25] Richard N. Longenecker, *Galatians*, Word Biblical Commentary 41 (Dallas: Word Biblical Commentary, 1990), 91.

A funny thing happened on the way to the forum, as it were, as the first century rolled into the second. People engaged in leadership have a way of thinking that leadership is the first among equals of ministries. It doesn't take long for the "among equals" to fade from sight. The result is fairly consistent: leaders take over the whole operation and think they own it. This is pretty much what happened in the church's Tradition. At times some church leaders, those who had proclaimed an unequivocal yes to God's vocation, focused attention on the church's leadership in order to safeguard and promote unity and to protect the community from heresy. Other leaders, with more mixed motives, were only too happy to amass power for themselves at the expense of the rest of the community. And yet others misunderstood the catholic character of ministry and inadvertently confirmed the monopoly of ministry on what became the clergy.

As hard as it may be to believe, the first-century Christian Tradition was completely oblivious to the distinction between clergy, that is, the leader, and laity, that is, the led. Slowly but surely, various communities adopted the method of the ministry of leadership described in the Pastoral Epistles, the Acts of the Apostles, and 1 Peter. Their ministry was primarily administrative, charged especially to keep the communities true to the faith passed on to them through the first generation of Christians. In fact, 1 Corinthians 12:28 even mentions a charism of administration[26]—distinct from the appointment of apostles. In this sense these ministers bore a great responsibility for the apostolicity of the church, that is, for nourishing the faith handed on by the "apostles." This responsibility was eventually expressed in the term *apostolic succession,* that is, something passed on from the apostles.

Chapter 3 of the Vatican II document *Lumen gentium,* "On the Hierarchical Structure of the Church and in Particular on the Episcopate," expresses a common understanding

---

[26] *Kubernesis,* meaning "to pilot or steer." It was metaphorically applied to government.

among Catholics of the development of the hierarchy in the first century. The council affirms that right from the period after Jesus's resurrection all members of the church have been participating in Jesus's ministry of priest, prophet, and king. It then goes on to speak about the ministry of the episcopacy. The bishops recognize that their ministry is the care of other members of the church in order to promote the evolution of salvation. The council's understanding of the origin of the bishops and of the church to which they minister may give the incorrect impression that the way ministry in the church is now structured was directly mandated by Christ. One might further get the impression that the first Christians in the New Testament established this structure for all time. What actually happened, though, far more resembles the process of natural evolution than a divine edict.

For starters, the council states that Jesus "established" the church (*LG* 12). He did, of course, but not in the same way that Mark Zuckerberg established Facebook. The church community has been around and evolving since God began calling people together. It took a quantum leap forward through Jesus's life, death, and resurrection. Through Christ creation enters into the final stage of evolution: salvation, the fullness of reality, communion with God and with all other creatures. But Jesus did not establish an institution with a constitution, laws, bylaws, and a divinely decreed organizational structure.[27] Scripture scholars agree that there is no evidence that the historical Jesus intended to establish anything but the kingdom of God. And there is no evidence that he knew exactly what that kingdom would look like other than the community of all humankind with God. The New Testament, especially Jesus's discourse in Matthew 18, indicates how the early church was inspired by Jesus's life and ministry to establish and organize itself. Any claim that Jesus gave instructions for how the church was to be organized in perpetuity rather than participate in

---

[27] See Rémi Parent and Simon Dufour, *Les Ministères* (Québec: Éditions Paulines, 1993), 28ff.

natural evolution would appear to violate the very natural law that God established. The entire universe, including the church, is evolving and constantly changing. There is no scientific evidence, indeed, no evidence of any kind, that God decreed any kind of specific organization for anything. And we have seen that the organizational structure of the church did, in fact, change, even in the first century.

Another headache is getting clear who the apostles were and what their ministry was. We know that Jesus called twelve men to accompany him during his public ministry (Matt 10:2–4; Mark 3:16–19; Luke 6:12–19; Acts 1:13). This group became known as the Twelve. The number twelve is highly significant. It indicates that the early Christians somehow understood these twelve as fulfilling Israel's longing for the reconstitution of the twelve tribes of Israel. That reconstitution was an indication of the fulfillment of salvation history, the eschaton. As we know, one of the Twelve, Judas, betrayed Jesus and one way or another dropped out of the club. Acts 1:15–26 tells the story of how the risen Lord, through the medium of throwing lots, called a replacement for Judas: Matthias. They did this so that the Twelve would not be tainted with disintegration through Judas's sin but be a symbol of the eschaton. Notice, however, that there is no indication that anyone was ever elected again to join the Twelve after they began to die off. In fact, we don't know what happened to a good number of them.

Apostle describes a different kind of ministry from the Twelve, though the two are not mutually exclusive. *Apostle* comes from the Greek word *to send*, so apostles were actually missionaries. Some of the Twelve did become apostles—most notably, of course, Peter—but most did not. On the other hand, most of the apostles were not members of the Twelve, including Paul and Barnabas. The Twelve, however, had a good amount of moral authority. For example, they seem to have had a role in approving missionary endeavors.[28] Missionaries, of course,

---

[28] Raymond Brown, SS, *Priest and Bishop: Biblical Reflections* (Paramus, NJ: Paulist Press, 1970), 51.

tend to move around and generally don't have the charism of administration. Paul recognizes this in 1 Corinthians 12:28, where he lists the charism of administration separately from the apostles.

Now that we've sorted out the different ministries of the Twelve and apostles, what about the bishops? The New Testament uses two Greek words to describe what certainly appears to be the same ministry. One is *episkopos,* which means "overseer," and the other *presbuteros*, which means "elder." The word *episkopos* morphed into *bishop* in English after passing through a number of languages and losing the initial *e-* and the concluding *-os. Presbuteros* took not only a linguistic journey but also a theological one. Once the community decided that the *episkopos* or *presbuteros* would preside at the Eucharist, a decision that came in some communities toward the end of the first century (there's no evidence that they did so in the New Testament) and once a sacrificial character became associated with the Eucharist, the *presbuteros* became a priest. Why? Because priests offer sacrifice. More on that later. We need to be careful here, though. The New Testament itself never understood the ministry of the *presbuteros* to be any more priestly than any other Christian. The Greek word for "priest" is completely different: *hiereus.* The New Testament *presbuteros*, therefore, is better translated as "presbyter" rather than "priest." The English translations of *Lumen gentium* and of the council's document on the priesthood, *Presbyterorum ordinis*, are misleading. The English translation incorrectly renders the Latin word *presbyterus* as "priest." The Latin text of both documents consistently uses the word *presbyterus*, a word borrowed from Greek meaning "elder." The Latin word for priest is *sacerdos.* After the fourth of seven drafts of *Presbyterorum ordinis,* all occurrences of *sacerdos* as referring to a minister were changed to *presbyterus.* It would appear that the council wanted to deemphasize the sacerdotal or priestly character of the ministry of presbyter.[29] Such a deemphasis

---

[29] Parent and Dufour, *Les Ministères*, 63.

serves to reemphasize the priestly character of the ministry of all members of the church.

Were any of the Twelve or the apostles bishops or presbyters? Probably not. The charisms for these ministries are very different. The description of the character traits of a bishop or presbyter in the Pastoral Epistles would certainly appear to disqualify Paul himself.[30] Although Peter is traditionally called the first bishop of Rome, Raymond Brown finds such a description "quite unlikely." Brown cites church historian D. W. O'Connor:

> That Peter founded the church at Rome is extremely doubtful and that he served as its first bishop (as we understand the term today) for even one year, much less the twenty-five-year period that is claimed for him, is an unfounded tradition that can be traced back to a point no earlier than the third century.[31]

We find a similar situation in other places with Christian communities, such that Brown concludes that the Twelve, apostles, and bishops-presbyters were different ministries that existed side by side.[32]

Lumen gentium expresses the common understanding that the twelve apostles appointed their successors as bishops. The council makes this statement as a way of expressing the belief that Christ's mission to "preach the kingdom of God" continues faithfully in the church:

> That divine mission, entrusted by Christ to the apostles, will last until the end of the world (cf. Mt. 28:20), since the Gospel they are to teach is for all time the source of all life for the Church. And for this reason the apostles, appointed as rulers in this society, took care to appoint successors. (*LG* 20)

---

[30] Brown, *Priest and Bishop*, 35.

[31] D. W. O'Connor, *Peter in Rome* (New York: Columbia University Press, 1969), 207. Cited in Brown, *Priest and Bishop*, 53.

[32] Brown, *Priest and Bishop*, 54.

The text refers to the witness of Saint Irenaeus of Lyons, who held that "through those who were appointed bishops by the apostles, and through their successors down in our own time, the apostolic tradition is manifested and preserved." *Lumen gentium* concludes: "Therefore, the Sacred Council teaches that bishops by divine institution have succeeded to the place of the apostles, as shepherds of the Church, and he who hears them, hears Christ, and he who rejects them, rejects Christ and Him who sent Christ."

The theological insight expressed by the council is sound: God works through people to promote the kingdom of God, the fulfillment of the universe's evolution. In this sense the ministry of bishop is "by divine institution." It is divinely instituted through the natural evolution of the church. This is the way people find appropriate forms of ministry to actualize the energy of the Holy Spirit for the promotion of salvation. It would be wrong, however, to conclude that God "instituted" any ministry directly, telling people what to do in perpetuity. Irenaeus's witness supports the theological contention that the bishops served to "manifest and preserve" the faith handed down through the apostles. As a historical witness of what happened during the time of the New Testament, however, Irenaeus isn't particularly trustworthy; he lived in the second century, born approximately one hundred years after Jesus's death.

The Development of Ministry after the First Century

The story of the development of ministry after the close of the New Testament was written by that mix of people I spoke of earlier—those whose intentions ranged from good to bad to something in between. There were people who seemed genuinely inspired by the Holy Spirit and promoted catholic forms of ministry well adapted to their times and places. Some representatives of this group are those people known as the fathers of the church; the desert mothers and fathers; founders of monastic movements, Francis of Assisi and Dominic de Guzmán; many of the Reformers of the sixteenth century; and founders of lay and religious movements in the Catholic Church during and after the Reformation and French Revolution. Others saw an increasingly powerful Christian community as a means of self advancement. They cared little for ministry. This movement started with Simon Magus in Acts 8:9–24 and strikingly flourished in many medieval and Renaissance popes and bishops. Most people just did their best to respond to the divine vocation to cooperate with God in the history of salvation with a mixture of motivations. The pattern thus corresponds exactly to that of evolution as described by scientists. Through the sacraments of initiation Christians pass from the old natural order characterized by a mixture of selfishness and altruism into the new natural order characterized by the selfless love that is God. We are saints—but not yet. There's still work to be done to complete "what is lacking in Christ's afflictions for the sake of his body, that is, the church" (Col 1:24). The church is still in the process of dying to the old order tainted by sin and rising to the new order of universal love. The history of salvation is the history of natural selection, inspired by the Holy Spirit and carried out by people who are simultaneously saints and sinners. We see this pattern in the history of the development of ministry in Christianity.

Thomas F. O'Meara, OP, identifies six stages in what he calls the "metamorphoses of ministry":

(1) a move through communal diversity and universality to a small number of ministries with prominence given to the service of leadership (episcopization) along with a further presentation of the ministry of leadership (presbyter or bishop) as a priest (sacerdotalization); (2) the absorption by the monastery of ministry and spirituality (monasticization); (3) a dominance of one philosophical-social structure in the cluster of offices (hierarchization); (4) the interlude of the Reformation (pastoralization of ministry)—a movement that is antimonastic and antipriestly but still reductionist; (5) the

Counter-Reformation's organization of ministry along the lines of the Baroque papacy and Baroque spirituality; (6) the romanticization of the ministry in the nineteenth century.[33]

Except for the fourth period (the Reformation), all attention after the first period is on leadership and the transcendent. Some of this emphasis in theology and church history on ministry as leadership may be due to the kind of people who wrote the texts: leaders. History is written by the victors, or at least those in power. To what degree the activities of laypeople were thought of as ministries is difficult to tell. Did medieval serfs make a connection between their work and their prayer when the angelus rang? How did laypeople understand hearing confessions and anointing the sick when such was still permitted? Why are there plaques of people engaged in nonclerical activity on the bell tower of the cathedral of Florence? Perhaps at some level they sensed that their work was ministry, promoting the welfare of the community, which is the church.

In any case, the texts available to us trace the development of ministry as one of leadership carried out increasingly by a specific group of people within the church: clerics. By the end of the first century, leadership was exercised by those called presbyter-bishops, primarily among Jewish-Christians, and those called deacons, among Hellenistic Christians.[34] As times and needs evolved, so did ministry. Canadian theologians Rémi Parent and Simon Dufour identify three factors in the late first century that prompted Christians to adapt their forms of leadership: the danger of schism, persecution, and the growth of cities.[35] The result was the development of the monarchical bishop to which *Lumen gentium* refers when speaking of the second-century writer Irenaeus of Lyons. In fact, Irenaeus's

---

[33] Thomas F. O'Meara, OP, *Theology of Ministry*, completely rev. ed. (New York: Paulist Press, 1999), 88–89.

[34] Parent and Dufour, *Les Ministères*, 36.

[35] Ibid., 40.

work (which the document cites) is titled *Adversus haereses (Against Heresies)*. Ignatius of Antioch in the late first century answered the challenge to the unity of the church with a curious variation on Irenaeus's idea. Irenaeus had written: "Where the Church is, there also is the Spirit of God; and where the Spirit of God is, there is the Church and all grace. And the Spirit is Truth."[36] Ignatius, on the other hand, puts the bishop where Irenaeus had put the Holy Spirit. Ignatius emphasized that the bishop served not only as the symbol of the church's unity but of the church itself: "Wheresoever the bishop shall appear, there let the people be; even as where Jesus may be, there is the universal Church. It is not lawful apart from the bishop either to baptize or to hold a love-feast; but whatsoever he shall approve, this is well-pleasing also to God; that everything which ye do may be sure and valid."[37] The bishop in Ignatius plays the role of the Holy Spirit in Irenaeus. Cyprian of Carthage in the third century expanded on Ignatius's idea of the church by linking it to the power that Jesus gave to Peter. According to Cyprian, Peter then shared that power with the other apostles after the resurrection. In his mind bishops participate in the same episcopacy, which has its source in Peter.

During the third and fourth centuries there was a tendency to sacerdotalize leadership, as mentioned above. An association was made especially with the priesthood in the Old Testament, thus conferring on Christian priests the role of mediator between God and the laity. Alas, the priesthood of the entire community, the body of Christ, faded into the background. Next, a theology of ordination developed that tended to emphasize the ritual or liturgical role of leaders. As time went on, ordination didn't so much recognize that the people getting ordained *had* the charism for the ministry they were going to undertake, but that ordination actually *gave* them the charism.

---

[36] PG, vol. 7, part 1, 966.
[37] "Letter to the Smyrnaeans," *Apostolic Fathers* (Lightfoot and Harmer: 1891), 8.

The fourth century marks a decisive turning point for Christianity and its understanding of ministry. In 313 Emperor Constantine lifted all restrictions on Christianity. The official version of the story of why he did that involves a vision of the cross under whose banner he was assured that he would slaughter his enemies. Sounds suspect. In any case, Constantine hitched his political star to the tenacious and growing Christian community. Sixty-seven years later, in 380, the emperors Gratian, Valentinian II, and Theodosius issued the decree *Cunctos populos,* making the Christian faith as defined by the Council of Nicaea the official *religio* of the Roman Empire. Recall that *religio* is best not translated as "religion" in ancient texts.[38] Nicaean Christianity became the official culture of the empire. Christian leaders became equated with priests of the ancien régime. The word *ecclesia* (church) became more identified with buildings than with the community. It is where the Christian priests offered the sacrifice of the Eucharist. Leaders were also incorporated into a private club (the clergy) that operated fairly independently of the laity.

As the *religio* of the empire, Christianity began to bump up against some thorny questions with regard to the role of the emperor. In the old days the emperor was clearly the head of the Roman *religio,* that is to say, Roman culture. The Christian clergy developed along the lines of the hierarchical structure of the old Roman *religio.* For better or for worse, the Christian confrontation with the ancien régime in the West was minimal thanks to the collapse of the Western empire. Bishops, abbots, and abbesses began wearing tiaras or crowns as symbols of their power and authority. The bishops of Rome began wearing tiaras in the ninth century; Eastern bishops started wearing them after the fall of Constantinople in 1453. The miters that Western bishops wear are variations of the tiara. The monarchical model of leader developed even further with the eleventh century "investiture controversy" and the Gregorian Reform.

---

[38] See the Introduction to this book for a discussion of the changing definitions of the word *religion.*

This controversy centered around who was the real boss in the Christian *religio*: the nobility or the clergy? In a sense this controversy had been festering for centuries, but because of a power vacuum the clergy had become dominant. Kings and emperors got their authority from God through the clergy. Pope Gregory VII, a former abbot of Cluny with plenty of experience in centralizing power for the good of the community, applied the same technique when he became pope as he had when he was an abbot. He centralized power in Rome. In 1075 he issued the *Dictatus papae*, in which he made it perfectly clear that the pope was boss. Authority flowed through the pope. The clergy were responsible to him alone. The function of the laity was basically to receive the sacraments from the clergy and to support the clergy. The nobility certainly didn't give up without a fight. The Cathedral of Monreale in Sicily, for example, contains twelfth-century mosaics of King Guglielmo. In one he is portrayed as being crowned king by Christ; in another he is offering the church to Mary. No clergy are in sight. On the other hand, a thirteenth-century series of frescoes in the Roman church of Santi Quattro Coronati shows Emperor Constantine acknowledging the authority of Pope Sylvester.

The sacerdotalization of priests with its ensuing monopolization of ministry was aided by the spread of the Christian community from large cities to towns and villages. Bishops remained in the cities and sent priests into the countryside. Their main task was to say mass, and they began to be called priests of the second order. To support themselves, these priests accepted stipends for saying mass. It occurred to these priests that they could say mass and earn stipends without the bother of a congregation, and thus the private mass was born.

Finally, theologians developed a theory about the *character* of the clergy. We find the idea of character developed by Saint Augustine in order to counter the arguments of a group called Donatists. The Donatists claimed that people who had committed apostasy, that is, denied the faith during the Roman persecutions, had to be rebaptized, and that sacraments celebrated by priests who had apostatized were not valid. Augustine, who isn't called the Doctor of Grace for nothing, argued that both baptism and ordination were gifts from God that could not be lost. He taught that they conferred a permanent character or seal on the person as a way of explaining that there was no need to repeat them in order to receive that grace again. Saint Thomas Aquinas further developed this theory.[39] For Thomas, the character or seal incorporates a person into the clergy.[40]

The theology of the character conferred by ordination onto priests is related to a concept first developed by the fathers of the church. They described a priest as acting *in persona Christi* (in the person of Christ). They did so to express their belief that the priest acted as an agent or minister of the whole church, the body of Christ. They got the expression—*en prosôpô Christoû*— from 2 Corinthians 2:10. Modern English Bibles translate this as "in the presence of Christ," but the fathers of the church took their cue from the Latin translation *in persona Christi*. Thomas Aquinas made a link between this expression and consecration at the Eucharist. He did so to emphasize that the whole church, the body of Christ, participates in the consecration. The priest serves as a symbol of the whole community celebrating the sacrament. When the priest is in communion with the church, he also celebrates the Eucharist *in persona ecclesiae* (in the person of the church). The church, after all, is the body of Christ. Thomas then went on to explain that a priest who is separated from the church can still validly consecrate the bread and wine at the Eucharist because he does so *in persona Christi* even if not *in persona ecclesiae*. The priest acts as an agent of Christ but not of the church. He did this for the same reason that Augustine did: a priest's ministry is from God and not dependent on the state of his soul. There is no way to judge just how holy a priest has to be for the sacraments he

---

[39] Thomas Aquinas, *Summa Theologica* III q. 63 a. 3.

[40] Thomas Aquinas, *Summa Theologica* Supplement q. 34 a. 2 obj. 1. See further Edward Schillebeeckx, "Theologische kanttekeningen bij de huidige priester-crisis," *Tijdschrift voor Theologie* 8 (1968): 402–34.

celebrates to be real. They are real because the priest is validly ordained *(ex opere operantis)* and he performs the rite correctly *(ex opere operato)*. Unfortunately, however, Thomas separated the essential link between a priest's ministry and the church. Now he could be a free agent, if an illegal one, without acting as an agent of the church.[41] He is an *alter Christus*, "another Christ," simply by the power of ordination. In time, however, the expression became synonymous with *in nomine Christi* in the sense of a delegate of Christ who, through ordination, is "conformed" to Christ.[42] Pope John Paul II's 1992 Apostolic Exhortation *Pastores dabos vos* thus logically asserts that through the sacrament of holy orders, "as a sacrament proper and specific to the priest [presbyter], and thus involving a new consecration to God through ordination," the presbyter is configured "to Christ, the head and shepherd of the church" and shares in the mission of "preaching the good news to the poor" "in the name and in the person of him who is head and shepherd of the Church." His very identity is to "continue the life and activity of Christ himself" *(Pastores dabo vobis* 18–20).[43]

Pope Benedict XVI, in a General Audience at Saint Peter's Square, June 24, 2009, explained that the priest as *alter Christus* is "configured to Christ ontologically, acquires an essentially relational character: he is in Christ, for Christ and with Christ, at the service of humankind." *Ontological configuration* is a term from metaphysics, the branch of philosophy that deals with being, substance, and the cause of things. The

---

[41] Bernard Dominique Marliangeas, *Clés pour une théologie du ministère: In persona Christi, in persona Ecclesiae,* in Théologie historique 51 (Paris: Beauchesne, 1978). See further David N. Power, "Representing Christ in Community and Sacrament," *Being a Priest Today*, Donald J. Goergen, OP, ed. (Collegeville, MN: Glazier, 1992), 97–123.

[42] Marliangeas, "Clés pour une théologie du ministère." The Vatican II document *Presbyterorum ordinis* uses this language, as does Pope John Paul II's 1992 Apostolic Exhortation *Pastores dabo vobis.*

[43] The document seems to use the words *sacerdotes* and *presbyter* interchangeably.

pope is building on a statement about the character of priests from Vatican II.

The Vatican II document *Lumen gentium* uses the theology of metaphysics and character to describe how ordained ministers differ from those who are not ordained:

> Though they differ from one another in essence and not only in degree, the common priesthood of the faithful and the ministerial or hierarchical priesthood are nonetheless interrelated: each of them in its own special way is a participation in the one priesthood of Christ. The ministerial priest, by the sacred power he enjoys, teaches and rules the priestly people; acting in the person of Christ, he makes present the Eucharistic sacrifice, and offers it to God in the name of all the people. But the faithful, in virtue of their royal priesthood, join in the offering of the Eucharist. They likewise exercise that priesthood in receiving the sacraments, in prayer and thanksgiving, in the witness of a holy life, and by self-denial and active charity. (*LG* 10)

The council describes the distinction between the clergy and the laity in the strongest terms. Thomas Aquinas, basing himself on Aristotle, understood *essence* to mean the nature of something, that which makes it what it is. The council sees a profound difference between the priesthood that it describes as "ministerial or hierarchical" and everyone else.

Subsequent teachings of the church's magisterium have underlined the difference that the council saw. We see this in Pope John Paul II's 1988 Apostolic Exhortation *Christifideles laici*, his 1994 intervention at the symposium on *The Participation of the Lay Faithful in the Priestly Ministry*, and his 1997 instruction *On Certain Questions Regarding the Collaboration of the Non-Ordained Faithful in the Sacred Ministry of Priests*. The pope struggles to distinguish the theology as well as the vocabulary that describe the work of the clergy and the laity. He does so "from the need to be obedient to the will of

Christ and to respect the constitutive form which he indelibly impressed on his Church."[44] That form, he explains, flows from the ontological difference between the ways the clergy and the laity participate in the one priesthood of Christ. The clergy engage in sacred ministry, and the laity engage in secular tasks. The laity may, on occasion, participate in the clergy's ministry, but the pope emphasizes that what the laity does in such cases does not qualify them as sacred ministers.

In 2006 Cardinal Avery Dulles noted that since the Middle Ages official documents did not refer to a mission or ministry for the laity. Such terms were reserved for the clergy. Vatican II changed that restriction as it recognized that all Christians by virtue of baptism share in Christ's offices of priest, prophet, and king. As noted, however, the laity were seen as having a secular calling: "to engage in temporal affairs, seeking to order them according to the plan of God." Under the influence of vocabulary from Catholic Action, Dulles explains, the council used the word *apostolate* to refer to the work of the laity. *Apostolicam actuositatem* states: "All activity of the Mystical Body directed to the attainment of this goal [the spread of the kingdom of God] is called the apostolate, which the Church carries on in various ways through all her members" (*AA* 2). The council understands baptism and confirmation as the way the laity is commissioned to the apostolate. The council, Dulles notes, realized the ambiguity of assigning a "secular" characterization to the work of the laity, since not all laity are engaged in secular endeavors and many priests are.[45]

The council does occasionally use the word *ministry* in connection with the laity, as when referring to liturgical functions

---

[44] Pope John Paul II, *Discourse at the Symposium on "The Participation of the Lay Faithful in the Priestly Ministry"* (May 11, 1994), 3. John Paul II uses the quotation in *On Certain Questions Regarding the Collaboration of the Non-Ordained Faithful in the Sacred Ministry of Priest* (1997).

[45] Cardinal Avery Dulles, "Can Laity Properly Be Called 'Ministers'?" *Origins* 35 (April 20, 2006): 726–31.

(*Sacrosanctum concilium* 29), Christian education (*Gravissimum educationis* 7, 8), and missionary work (*Ad gentes* 26). *Gaudium et spes* uses the word *ministerium* most often, referring to any kind of service laypeople perform, including work for peace and justice. Dulles does not think that the reservation of the terms *minister* and *ministry* to clergy is warranted by scripture or Tradition. He believes that the Bible uses the terms that are translated as "ministry" for all activities that promote the life of the community, and that since the council there has been a tendency to expand the use of the word to the laity.[46] In 1972, Pope Paul VI established the "lay ministries" of lector and acolyte and invited episcopal conferences to submit requests for more. The invitation, Dulles reports, was "generally ignored." In Pope Paul VI's 1975 Apostolic Exhortation *Evangelii nuntiandi* the pope writes:

> The laity can also feel called, or in fact be called, to cooperate with their pastors in the service of the ecclesial community for the sake of its growth and life. This can be done through the exercise of different kinds of ministries according to the grace and charisms which the Lord has been pleased to bestow on them. (*EN* 73)

In 1981 in *Familiaris consortio* John Paul II referred to "the ministry of evangelization" that parents exercise with their families (*FC* 4). In *Christifideles laici*, in 1988, he acknowledges "the ministries, offices and roles of the lay faithful that find their foundation in the sacraments of baptism and confirmation" (*CL* 23), though he warns that the use of the word *ministry* should not clericalize the laity. Finally, in 2001 the pope wrote in *Novo millennio ineunte*:

> Together with the ordained ministry, other ministries, whether formally instituted or simply recognized, can

---

[46] Ibid., 728.

flourish for the good of the whole community, sustaining it in all its many needs: from catechesis to liturgy, from the education of the young to the widest array of charitable works. (*NM* 46)

The United States Conference of Catholic Bishops also calls the work of the laity "ministry" in its 1980 document *Called and Gifted*; in the 1995 document *Called and Gifted for the New Millennium*; and in the 2005 document *Co-Workers in the Vineyard*.

Dulles opines that although some ministry should be reserved to the clergy alone, the laity "have a ministry to build up the church" under the hierarchy's supervision. Vatican II wanted to integrate faith and daily life (*Gaudium et spes* 43). Dulles concludes:

> It would be a mistake, I believe, to make a sharp dichotomy between ministry in the church and apostolate in the world, as if it were necessary to choose between them. Lay ministries in the church, properly conducted, can greatly help to offset the forces of secularism; they can form a Catholic people sufficiently united to Christ in prayer and sufficiently firm and well instructed in their faith to carry out the kinds of apostolate that Vatican II envisaged.[47]

Dulles seems to sense the artificiality of distinguishing two spheres of reality, the sacred and the secular. Thus, while acknowledging that not all laypeople can engage successfully in all ministries, he does call for the recognition of the catholicity of ministry. The great variety of ministries in which laypeople engage promotes the establishment of the kingdom of God. Dulles notes regretfully, however, that "the council's hopes that the lay faithful would find new motivation for evangelizing the world and transforming the temporal order according to the

---

[47] Ibid., 730.

plan of God remain largely unfulfilled."[48] The next chapter will critique the theology of ministry that has developed in church Tradition. This critique may offer insights into why the council's hopes have not been fulfilled, and what we can do about it.

---

[48] Ibid.

Chapter 4

A Critique of Ministry in the Church's Tradition

Our quick tour of two thousand years of the church's tradition of ministry, starting with the Bible itself, has, I hope, provided a sketch of how Christians, energized by the Holy Spirit, developed ministry for the purpose of promoting the evolution of the universe into the kingdom of God. The history reveals a pattern, a process that followed the law of natural selection. Various forms of ministry developed within human culture as we adapted to changing environments. As always happens in evolution, some mutations—in this case experiments in cultural adaptation—have developed for the good of the community but then became extinct when they lost their usefulness or evolved into something else that proved useful. The Twelve served their purpose and then died out. Presbyter-bishops developed into two different ministries. Deacons evolved from the equivalent of presbyter-bishops in Gentile communities into helpers first of bishops and then also of priests.

The Western or "Catholic" Church has excelled in promoting unity but, ironically, at the cost of underemphasizing catholicity. The opposite is true of the ecclesiology of the Orthodox Church, which consists of autocephalous or quasi-independent national churches with no central authority equivalent to the papacy. To preserve and promote unity and apostolicity both churches have fairly consistently limited their understanding of ministry to what the clergy does. The church is weak on recognizing that all Christians engage in various—catholic—forms of ministry. Ministry is one of the ways by which people grow in the church's holiness. It's also how people contribute to the church's holiness. It's a way of expressing their love, energized by the Holy Spirit. By our nature as the people of God we are creatures whom God calls and animates to grow in holiness. God made us to love, which includes expressing love through action, that is, through ministry.

Let's critique the tradition that we have sketched in light of what we have learned about the evolution of salvation history. Our critique will ask what aspects of ministry in the tradition have promoted or hindered people's ability to express love in action. How has the tradition helped people to be co-creators with God in promoting salvation history? How has the tradition helped or frustrated people's participation in the evolutionary process that brings the universe to fulfillment? As we've seen, evolution through natural selection depends on environmental change, physical mutation, selfish behavior, and altruistic behavior. These days, for us humans this process is occurring mainly through biocultural evolution. And as we've said, this "cultural" evolution is how people respond to the transcendent vocation to be co-creators of the kingdom of God.[1] The task of *religio* is to help people, to guide people, to enable people to make good responses to that vocation.[2] Let's evaluate how well the Christian *religio* in the West is doing that.

Baptism: The Origin of Ministry

The first words out of Jesus's mouth as reported in Mark's Gospel—the first of the Gospels to be written—are: "'The

---

[1] See Philip Hefner, "Biocultural Evolution and the Created Co-Creator," *Dialog* 36 (1997): 197–205.

[2] Philip Hefner, "The Spiritual Task of Religion in Culture: An Evolutionary Perspective," *Zygon* 33 (1998): 535–44.

time is fulfilled, and the kingdom of God is at hand; repent and believe in the gospel'" (Mark 1:15). These words say it all. Christians see Jesus as the one fulfilling time. Greek has two words for time: *chronos* and *kairos*. *Chronos* refers to what we might call the immanent dimension of reality and *kairos* to the transcendent. Mark uses the word *kairos* here. He's expressing his belief that the history of salvation, the evolution of the universe toward its fulfillment, is completed in Christ. What should people do? "Repent and believe in the gospel." It's pretty much the same answer that Peter gives the crowd after his Pentecost speech in the Acts of the Apostles. There he describes how the people to whom he is speaking just made what at first sight looks like the worst mistake ever: they murdered their savior. In horror, "stung in their hearts," the people ask: "What may we do, brothers?" Peter answers: "repent and be baptized" (Acts 2:37–38).

"Repent" in these two texts is the translation of the Greek word *metánoia*. This word means a change of mind or heart. It involves a profound change in which we look at the world and how we act. So, what are Jesus and Peter telling us to do? What do we have to change from? The answer is remarkably simple: sin. We're born sinners. As we saw in Chapter 1, Christianity has come to call this condition original sin, which describes the selfish instincts with which we are born. We're not personally responsible for those instincts. In fact, without them we, as a species, wouldn't be here. Selfishness is one of the things that makes the world go around: it's essential to survival. It characterizes everything that exists and so, of itself, isn't bad. God makes the universe that way, and everything God makes is good. Yet Jesus and Peter are telling us to reject it. They want us to undergo the profound change of repentance, of *metánoia*. They want us to replace this behavior with belief in the gospel and baptism. What are they talking about?

First, let's clarify what sin is. Only creatures with conscience are capable of sin. Only creatures with conscience can be aware that there is a better way of living than one motivated, even partially, by selfishness. As far as I know, humans are the only creatures with a conscience. As noted in Chapter 3, like everything else about us, conscience is the product of natural selection in the process of evolution. We know that characteristics that develop through evolution perdure only when they are useful. Mutations, characteristics that arise naturally in the course of evolution, that are not useful die out with the individuals that have them. There must, therefore, be some evolutionary advantage to having a conscience; otherwise it would have died out. So, what is it good for?

Conscience is our capacity to know good from bad. All people have this capacity, and when we use it, we are attracted to acts of love. As we know from experience, it's not always easy to know what, exactly, those acts are, and we sometimes make mistakes. The Vatican II document *Gaudium et spes (Pastoral Constitution on the Church in the Modern World)* beautifully describes what conscience is and how and why it works:

> In the depths of his conscience, man detects a law which he does not impose upon himself, but which holds him to obedience. Always summoning him to love good and avoid evil, the voice of conscience when necessary speaks to his heart: do this, shun that. For man has in his heart a law written by God; to obey it is the very dignity of man; according to it he will be judged. Conscience is the most secret core and sanctuary of a man. There he is alone with God, Whose voice echoes in his depths. In a wonderful manner conscience reveals that law which is fulfilled by love of God and neighbor. In fidelity to conscience, Christians are joined with the rest of men in the search for truth, and for the genuine solution to the numerous problems which arise in the life of individuals from social relationships. Hence the more right conscience holds sway, the more persons and groups turn aside from blind choice and strive to be guided by the objective norms of morality. Conscience frequently errs from invincible ignorance without losing its dignity. The same cannot be said for a man who cares but little for truth and goodness,

or for a conscience which by degrees grows practically sightless as a result of habitual sin. (*GS* 10)

Conscience detects the "law" of love in the sense that Jesus commands love in John's Gospel. It is the "love of God and neighbor." Obeying this law is our "very dignity"; loving is how God creates us throughout our lives. Living love is the solution to the problems we encounter in our individual self and in our relations with other people. Conscience is our moral compass. It can err when we don't have all the information we need to make decisions, but as long as we keep trying, God will provide for our mistakes. People who don't care about promoting the good, however, engage in a process of self-destruction. Conscience indicates to us how to cooperate with God in establishing his kingdom. Conscience perceives the community of the Holy Trinity and offers guidance of how to live in such ways as to join it. "Joining" the Trinity is what the fathers of the church meant when they spoke of "deification," that is, incorporation into God.

Conscience lets us know about our selfish instincts. These instincts incline us to use the energy of the Holy Spirit in ways contrary to what our conscience tells us. The repentance to which Jesus and Peter call us is nothing more than listening to our conscience and rejecting sin. It's a profound change of attitude that strives to live love, to live altruism, to serve and cooperate with one another at any cost. Attitude can get us pretty far, but, alas, not far enough to live altruistic love all the time, like Jesus. A group called the Pelagians tried this in the fifth century. Saint Augustine pointed out the obvious: willpower alone isn't enough to make us saints.

Saint Paul's outburst in Romans 7:14–25 expresses the difference between knowing what is right, what we ought to do, and doing it. Paul recognizes that the Law of the Old Testament tells us how to live so as to join God. The trouble is, no one can do it because we are sinful; we have selfish, inherited instincts. "Wretched man that I am!" Paul cries out. "Who will rescue me from this body of death? Thanks be to God through

Jesus Christ." Paul expresses the experience of Christians as we recognize our slavery to sin and the way of liberation. Augustine elaborated the theology of grace to explain how Christ rescues us.

In Mark's Gospel Jesus indicates that the solution to sin, the way to repent, the way profoundly to change our attitude and our action, is to "believe in the gospel." Belief does not mean just saying yes to a bunch of theological statements. The etymology of the English word *believe* demonstrates how people have understood its deep meaning. It is a variation of a Proto-Indo-European root, *leubh-*, which means "to love." "Believe in the gospel" means love the good news that Jesus liberates us from the chains of sin. It means engage with Jesus, allow him to effect the transformation of repentance. Peter explains how: be baptized.

Baptism is the sacrament by which people literally die to the old order of sin and are reborn or raised to the new order of selfless love. Baptism is an expression of what theologians call *eschatological tension*. It's the tension that Paul described when, on the one hand, he wants to live love, live the kingdom of God here and now, and on the other hand, can't. It's the apparent contradictory statements Jesus makes when he says, "The kingdom of God is among [or within] you" (Luke 17:21), and all the parables about how the kingdom of God is still coming. Through baptism we have died with Christ and are raised with him to live a sinless life (Rom 6:1ff.). Yes, the "have died" and "are raised" take time in the immanent sense of *chronos*. It's a project in which we participate; it won't be finished until our physical death and resurrection. It's important to keep in mind that although Christians experience this sacrament of baptism by means of a specific ritual, all people are invited to the transformation it involves. All people who hear and obey conscience in their hearts do so by God's grace. They die with Christ and rise with him.

Baptism makes us acutely aware of God's call, vocation, to holiness. The Vatican II document *Lumen gentium* captures this experience beautifully, devoting all of chapter 5 to the universal call to holiness. The church is holy; this is one of its traditional marks, along with one, catholic, and apostolic. It is holy because it is the body of Christ—Christ who conquered sin through love and is the Way to universal fulfillment. The church's members are in the process of becoming holy, but eschatological tension rears its ugly head once again. The council rejoices in the grace that God provides to make the human response to God's vocation possible. And it recognizes that there are many paths to this holiness, all of which are expressions of love, of the energy that is the Holy Spirit drawing all creation into communion, to the ultimate resolution of eschatological tension. We need to work with God, to allow the Holy Spirit to animate and direct us, so that in Christ we transform creation into the kingdom of God. As Paul tells an uncooperative group of people in Corinth: "For the kingdom of God depends not on talk but on power" (1 Cor 4:20). The concluding meditation of *The Spiritual Exercises* of Saint Ignatius describes the expression of power of which Paul speaks: "Love ought to manifest itself in deeds rather than in words" and "love consists in mutual sharing of goods."

Evaluation of the Theology of Ministry in the Catholic Church Today

The description of ministry in the New Testament serves as a paradigm for a theology of ministry. It offers guidelines not so much on specifics of forms of ministry but rather on its character and purpose. From the New Testament we see that ministry is the manifestation of love; it is putting love into action. It is the way that we both live and develop the new life into which we were born through baptism. That life has the characteristics of the church itself: one, holy, catholic, and apostolic. By ministry we use the gifts, the charisms, that God gives us. God calls us to use our gifts for the common good and in diverse, catholic ways (1 Cor 12:7). Thomas O'Meara helps us to see more clearly the character of ministry gleaned from the first century: "Christian ministry is not sacral office. . . . Christian ministry is action that is service to the kingdom of God. . . . Christian ministry is universal and diverse."[3] The New Testament did not limit ministry to what post-Enlightenment culture would call religion. Ministry was an integral part of the Christian *religio*, that is, how people responded to God, fulfilled their duty and their right to promote the evolution of creation, that is, salvation history. Everyone was engaged in a myriad of forms of ministry. Ministry is a duty as it answers the divine invitation to be co-creators with God. It is a right because it is one way by which God works through people to bring us to sanctity.

The Catholic Church in the twenty-first century under-stands and structures ministry, quite naturally, as it has been bequeathed to it from the past. That the Catholic *religio* is very much alive and well says something about how well that un-derstanding and ministry have worked. Is there any reason to change them? As the saying goes, if it isn't broken, don't fix it.

But there are data that suggest that the time for a reconsid-eration of ministry has arrived, at least in some parts of the world. In an essay based upon her participation in a Lilly fac-ulty seminar at Loyola University of Chicago, Mary Elsbernd, OSF, reports data on the aspirations and frustrations of stu-dents enrolled in the university's master of divinity program.[4] The students described their experiences of vocation as coming from the depths of their soul. They experienced God calling them to participate in God's work of creation by using their talents, and they desired to respond positively. Elsbernd writes: "These persons encountered God and entered into a relation-ship with God that needed to be made public or expressed." Likewise, "For a few, the transformation was not transition

---

[3] Thomas F. O'Meara, OP, *Theology of Ministry*, completely rev. ed. (New York: Paulist Press, 1999), 74–76.

[4] Mary Elsbernd, OSF, "Listening to a Life's Work: Contemporary Callings to Ministry," in *Revisiting the Idea of Vocation: Theological Explorations*, ed. John C. Haughey, SJ (Washington, DC: Catholic University of America Press, 2004), 196–219.

into ministry but consisted in getting the name ministry into their life work."[5] The students were happy to have an expanded understanding of vocation, which has traditionally been limited to the clergy and religious life.

The lack of Catholic ordained ministers in many parts of the world contrasts with the aspirations of laypeople. It suggests that a revised understanding of ministry is in order. Data from the Center for Applied Research in the Apostolate at Georgetown University demonstrate the decline in the number of ordained ministers in the United States and the increase in the Catholic population.[6]

The data reported by Mary Elsbernd mirror the interest in ecclesial ministry throughout North America, as witnessed by the number of laypeople studying in seminaries and theological schools. In many schools of theology laypeople outnumber seminarians preparing for ordination. The need for more ecclesial ministers that the data from the Center for Applied Research indicate seems to find a solution in the desire for more people to engage in ecclesial ministry. That all members of the church have a contribution to make is recognized by Vatican II: "In virtue of this catholicity each individual part [of the church] contributes through its special gifts to the good of the other parts and of the whole church. Through the common sharing of gifts and through the common effort to attain fullness in unity, the whole and each of the parts receive increase" (LG 13). So, what's wrong with this picture?

In order to evaluate how well catholicity is working in ministry in the church, let's take a look at the following theologies and practices: (1) the distinction between clergy and laity, (2) the character of ordination, (3) the distinction between sacred

---

[5] Ibid., 203, 206.

[6] A Le Moyne/Zogby International poll of American Catholics conducted March 7–10, 2005, revealed that 91.3% of those polled thought that it was important that laypeople play an active role in the church; 82.5% thought that baptism commits all Catholics to some form of ministry to promote the kingdom of God; and 74.8% considered their work a ministry.

and secular ministries, and (4) the church's hierarchical structure. In the process of our consideration we'll affirm what is good in these areas and offer suggestions for revision when they don't sufficiently promote catholicity.

The Distinction between Clergy and Laity

In 2007, a mini theological explosion occurred when the provincial council of the Order of Preachers (Dominicans) in the Netherlands issued a pamphlet entitled *Church and Ministry: Toward a Church with a Future.*[7] The pamphlet expresses pain and frustration that many Catholics are deprived of celebrating the Eucharist because of a lack of priests. It also makes note that, at least from the council's point of view, there is absolutely no lack of vocations to the priesthood. The problem is that most of the people who say that they have that vocation don't also have the vocation to celibacy or they're women. In 2008, at the request of the master general of the Order of Preachers in Rome, a French Dominican, Hervé Legrand, professor emeritus of the Institut Catholique in Paris, issued a response. He criticized a number of theological assertions and suggestions in the pamphlet but expressed sympathy for the reason it was written. In particular he expressed concern that "so many members of the people of God continue to wander like a flock without shepherds."[8] In 1984, Legrand had expressed the same concern for the church in France and warned against a solution that would just reinforce clericalism. He urged theologians to think creatively

---

[7] Originally published in Dutch as *Kerk en ambt. Onderweg naar een kerk met toekomst* (Nijmegen: Valkof Pers, 2007).

[8] "Rapport de l'ordre des dominicains concernant la brochure publiée aux Pays-Bas sur 'Ministères ordonnés et Eucharistie'" [*Lecture ecclésiologique faite à la demande du Maître de l'Ordre par le fr. Hervé Legrand op*] (January 7, 2008).

in order to adapt the church's theology and practice so as to be effective in contemporary Western society.[9]

Lumen gentium reaffirms the distinction between clergy and laity that in one form or another has existed in the church since the second century (no. 10). Aloys Grillmeier, a *peritus* or theological expert and adviser to the bishops at the council, reports that the way the council describes the distinction gives evidence of some tension and ambiguity among the bishops. The council described the difference between clergy and laity as one of "essence and not only in degree" because the council assumed that this distinction was real. It then had a hard time explaining it while also affirming the catholicity of ministry. Grillmeier enigmatically proposes that such a distinction was necessary "to avoid false interpretations."[10] but alas, he doesn't share with us what those false interpretations might have been. He does reveal that the council rejected a number of other proposed ways of distinguishing clergy from laity before it arrived at the one it finally accepted.[11] The council's formulation is pretty much lifted from an allocution of Pope Pius XII of 1954, *Magnificate Dominum*, where the pope discusses the role of the ordained minister and the layperson at the Eucharist. Grillmeier proposes: "The Constitution does not

---

[9] "Crise du clergé: hier et aujourd'hui. Essai de lecture ecclésiologique," *Lumière et vie* 33 (1984): 90–106.

[10] Aloys Grillmeier, "The People of God," in *Commentary on the Documents of Vatican II*, gen. ed. Herbert Vorgrimler, vol. 1 (New York: Herder and Herder, 1967), 157.

[11] Ibid., 157–58. He notes the following rejected proposals: (1) to minimize the common priesthood, calling it an "improper or initial *(inchoativum)* or a 'certain' priesthood which of itself did not merit the name"; (2) to acknowledge a "proper" character of the common priesthood seen as an "analogy" in order "to determine the dissimilarity while maintaining the similarity of the common and the special priesthood"; (3) to call the common priesthood the "spiritual priesthood" *(sacerdotium spirituale)* to distinguish it from the official priesthood; (4) to call it the "universal priesthood" *(sacerdotium universale)*.

claim to have found the definitive distinction. Its concern is to make a positive statement about the priesthood of the faithful while still keeping it apart from the consecrated priesthood."[12] If Grillmeier's interpretation is correct, then what the council wanted to do was point out that there is a difference in *function* between the clergy and laity. In that case the council was teaching that ordained ministers in the Catholic Church are not essentially different from anyone else, in that philosophical and metaphysical sense described in Chapter 3. Rather, the council was saying that ordained people join a group of ministers who have charisms that they exercise in essentially distinct ministries.[13] Furthermore, once a person is ordained into that group there is no need ever to join it again. We already saw this thinking when Augustine proposed the idea of a seal or character that comes with ordination.

Was the council right in assuming that the distinction between the clergy and the laity is "real"? Probably not or, at least, not all the time. The clergy-laity distinction was unknown to the New Testament Christian community. Only in the latter part of the second century do we find texts that clearly distinguish between something like clergy and laity. In fact, before the third century the organization and structure of ministries

---

[12] Ibid., 158.

[13] See Hervé-Marie Legrand, "The 'Indelible' Character and the Theology of Ministry," in *The Plurality of Ministries,* Concilium 74 (New York: Herder and Herder, 1974), 54–62; and Legrand, "Rapport de l'ordre des dominicains." Gary Macy notes that in the Middle Ages civic rulers were considered ordained. Gary Macy, *The Hidden History of Women's Ordination: Female Clergy in the Medieval West* (New York: Oxford University Press, 2008), 30. See also Yves Congar, "Note sur une valeur des termes 'ordinare, ordinatio,'" *Revue des sciences religieuses* 58 (1984): 7–14; Pierre-Marie Gy, "Les anciennes prières d'ordination," *La Maison-Dieu* 138 (1979): 93–122; Alexandre Faivre, *Ordonner la fraternité: Pouvoir d'innover et retour à l'ordre dans l'Église ancienne* (Paris: Cerf, 1992); and idem, *Les premiers laïcs: lorsque l'église naissait au monde* (Strasbourg: Éditions du Signe, 1999).

were so diverse in different parts of the church that we can't identify a single common denominator that is found in all of them.[14]

Clement of Rome, at the end of the first century, is the first Christian writer to use the word *layperson (laikós)*. He did so in his letter to the Corinthians, which is often cited as evidence that a class of laity existed already in the first century. Alexandre Faivre, a French theologian, thinks that Clement here is not speaking about Christians but Jews:

---

[14] See Faivre, *Ordonner la fraternité*; Edward Schillebeeckx, "Theologische kanttekeningen bij de huidige priester-crisis," *Tijdscrift voor Theologie* 8 (1968): 402–34; idem, "The Christian Community and Its Office-Bearers," in *The Right of the Community to a Priest*, ed. Edward Schillebeeckx and Johann-Baptist Metz, Concilium 133 (New York: Seabury, 1980), 95–133; idem, *The Church with a Human Face* (New York: Crossroad, 1985); Piet Fransen, SJ, "Orders and Ordination," in *Sacramentum Mundi: An Encyclopedia of Theology*, ed. Karl Rahner, SJ, et al., vol. 4 (New York: Herder and Herder, 1969); John McKenzie, "Ministerial Structures in the New Testament," in *The Plurality of Ministries*, Concilium 74 (New York: Herder and Herder, 1972), 13–22; Jean-Marie Tillard, "La 'qualité sacerdotale' du ministère chrétien," *Nouvelle Revue Théologique* 95 (1973): 481–514; Anton Houtepen, "Evangelie, kerk, ambt. Theologische diagnose van de huidige ambtsproblematiek," *Tijdschrift voor Theologie* 19 (1979): 235–52; F. Frost, "Ministère," in *Catholicisme. Hier, Aujourd'hui, Demain*, vol. 9 (Paris: Letouzey et Ané, 1982), 185–226; Thomas F. O'Meara, *Theology of Ministry*, 1st ed. (New York: Paulist Press, 1983), 80–138; idem, *Theology of Ministry*, 2nd ed. (New York: Paulist Press, 1999); Kenan B. Osborne, *Priesthood: A History of Ordained Ministry in the Roman Catholic Church*; idem, *Ministry: Lay Ministry in the Roman Catholic Church: Its History and Theology* (New York: Paulist Press, 1993); idem, "Envisioning a Theology of Ordained and Lay Ministry: Lay/Ordained Ministry–Current Issues of Ambiguity," in *Ordering the Baptismal Priesthood*, ed. Susan K. Wood (Collegeville, MN: Liturgical Press, 2003), 195–227; Jesús Álvarez Gómez, "La orden y el laicado: Experiencias, posibilidades," *Verdad y vida* 59 (2001): 409–36; Dean Flemming, "The Clergy/Laity Dichotomy: A New Testament Exegetical and Theological Analysis," *Asia Journal of Theology* 8 (1994): 232–50.

The *lay man* is therefore the type of man who believes he can find salvation in the cult of the old covenant. The term "lay" in this case is not so much pejorative as restrictive. It would refer to the man of the unfulfilled people. The man of that people who do not have access to the full spiritual knowledge which Christ introduces.[15]

Faivre concludes, therefore, that we cannot look to this early Christian writer for the distinction between cleric and lay.

We don't have any more luck finding a group of people classified as clerics in the first-century church either. The term *cleric* comes from the Greek word *klêros*. It referred to casting lots or dice and has a sense of "choice." It did not indicate a separate classification of people, ministers or otherwise. We find it, for example, in Acts 1:26 where the disciples "cast lots" to replace Judas by *choosing* Matthias to complete the Twelve. The New Testament also uses *klêros* to characterize all Christians in the sense that they are *chosen* for salvation. Ignatius of Antioch is the next witness to use the expression. For him, people are chosen for martyrdom—including himself.

The first time we come across the use of the term *clergy* in reference to a particular group of ministers in contrast to the laity is with the Latin-speaking, North African theologian Tertullian in the beginning of the third century.[16] Tertullian writes that the "clergy" exercise the ministries of leadership and unity, but that these are only two of the myriad ministries in the church. We suspect, by the way, that Tertullian himself was a layman. Tertullian clarifies that communion with the bishop may characterize the church, as Cyprian had said, but it does not constitute it:

---

[15] Faivre, *Les premiers laïcs*, 48.
[16] See ibid., 81–82; Osborne, *Ministry*, 37ff.; Houtepen, "Evangelie, kerk, ambt"; Schillebeeckx, "The Christian Community and Its Office-Bearers," 117.

For are not we laypeople also priests? It is written: "He has made us a kingdom and priests to God and his Father." It is ecclesiastical authority which distinguishes clergy and laity, this and the dignity which sets a man apart by reason of membership in the hierarchy. Hence where there is no such hierarchy you yourself offer sacrifice, you baptize and you are your own priest. Obviously where there are three gathered together even though they are lay persons there is a Church.[17]

The ministry of the clergy for Tertullian is leadership and unity, especially in the sacraments. Amazingly, he believes that the absence of the clergy does not mean that the community cannot celebrate the sacraments. There is no hint that he thinks in terms of difference in essence and not degree between the clergy and the laity, as *Lumen gentium* assumed. Tertullian's distinction appears to be based on the kinds of ministry each group did rather than on a group of ministers in contrast with Christians who do not do ministry. A Christian who does not do ministry is an oxymoron. The history of ministry in the church, therefore, knows of times when the distinction between clergy and laity did not exist. The distinction, therefore, is not essential.[18]

In a 1972 article, which he likens to Augustine's *Retractiones*, Yves Congar proposes that Catholic theology replace the categories of clergy and laity with those of ministry and modes

---

[17] *De castitatis* 7. English translation from *Tertullian: Treatises on Marriage and Remarriage: To His Wife, An Exhortation to Chastity, Monogamy*, trans. William P. Le Saint, Ancient Christian Writers (New York: Newman Press, 1951), 53. See further P. Van Beneden, "Het sacramenteel karakter van de ambtsverlening. Een terminologische studie in de christelijke latijnse literatuur vóór 313," *Tijdschrift voor Theologie* 8 (1968): 141–45.

[18] See further O'Meara, *Theology of Ministry*, 28–29, 167–98; Gary Macy, "The 'Invention' of Clergy and Laity in the Twelfth Century," in *A Sacramental Life: A Festschrift Honoring Bernard Cooke* (Milwaukee, WI: Marquette University Press, 2003), 117–35.

of community service. He expresses his vision as follows, "The Church of God is not built up solely by the actions of the official presbyteral ministry but by a multitude of diverse modes of service, stable or occasional, spontaneous or recognized, and, when the occasion arises, consecrated, while falling short of sacramental ordination."[19] His vision is consequent with the catholic model of church as communion in which all members actively participate in the communion's life according to their particular charisms.

The Character of Ordination

The third century witnessed the sacerdotalization of the clergy: bishops and presbyters became priests, and deacons became their special helpers. They became an *ordo*, a group of people within a hierarchy. This sacerdotalization now made clear just how the clergy differed from the laity. The ministry of the clergy focused on sacraments, especially the celebration of the Eucharist and the remission of sins.[20] Both Tertullian and the *Apostolic Tradition*, a document rediscovered only in the nineteenth century and dating from either the second or third century, give evidence of this development as both refer to the bishop as a high priest. What had started as a metaphorical use of sacerdotal vocabulary, as in the *Didachê* (13:3), eventually developed into the identity of the bishop-presbyter as a priest and the only person permitted to offer the Eucharist and remit sins. Jean-Marie Tillard proposes that the evolution from

---

[19] Yves Congar, "My Path-Findings in the Theology of Laity and Ministries," *The Jurist* 32 (1972): 176. See further Thomas O'Meara, "Le ministère dans l'église catholique d'aujourd'hui: les données de quelques trajectoires historiques," in *Des ministres pour l'Église,* ed. Joseph Doré and Maurice Vidal (Paris: Bayard/Centurion, 2002), 152–70.

[20] See Schillebeeckx, *The Church with a Human Face*, 141–44; Faivre, *Ordonner la fraternité*, 83.

this understanding of the priesthood of the communion to a separate *ordo* developed in a catechetical context. As Christians began to understand the Eucharist as a memorial of Jesus's sacrifice, they began to understand the person who presided at the Eucharist as a priest. It is the job of priests to offer sacrifice. Historically the emphasis on the sacrificial nature of the Eucharist began to develop after the destruction of the Temple in Jerusalem in 70 CE. Without the Temple it became even clearer that Jesus was the only high priest. The community recognized the words and gestures of the one who presided at the Eucharist as sacerdotal, which led to the designation of sacerdotal qualities to the presider.[21]

The evolution from recognizing sacerdotal qualities in the presider to identifying him as an *alter Christus* involved the evolution of the understanding of the expression *in persona Christi*, as we saw in Chapter 3. Bernard Dominique Marliangeas clarifies that Patristic writers correctly described the action of ordained Christian ministers or "priests" as done *in persona Christi*, because they understood it as an expression of an ecclesial act. Marliangeas notes that Patristic literature and then the Latin Vulgate translated the expression used in 2 Corinthians 2:10, *en prosôpô Christoû*, as "*in persona Christi*" due to a sacramental interpretation, even though the passage's context is not sacramental.[22] Early medieval liturgical texts tended to use both expressions *in* and *ex persona Christi* to indicate that the ministerial action was that of the whole church. In the thirteenth century Thomas Aquinas identified the use of the expression *in persona Christi* with the biblical words of consecration of the Eucharist but recognized that the whole church participates in that consecration. For him, therefore, *in*

---

[21] Tillard, "La 'qualité sacerdotale' du ministère chrétien." See also idem, *Dictionnaire de spiritualité ascétique et mystique*, "Sacerdoce"; and Fransen, "Orders and Ordination," 310.

[22] Bernard Dominique Marliangeas, *Clés pour une théologie du ministère: In persona Christi, in persona Ecclesiae*, Théologie historique 51 (Paris: Beauchesne, 1978).

persona Christi and *in persona Ecclesiae* expressed the same reality when referring to the eucharistic liturgy. The specific role of the minister is to act as an "organ" of the praying and believing community. As noted earlier, in order to emphasize the indelible character conferred by sacramental ordination, Thomas maintains that the minister who is separated from the unity of the church can still act *in persona Christi* but no longer *in persona ecclesiae*. This, of course, cleaves the essential relation between the minister's action as part of the life of the ecclesial communion. Henceforth the ordained minister had the power validly even if illicitly to celebrate the sacraments. That means that sacraments he celebrated were real but illegal. During the sixteenth century there developed a tendency to use the expression *in nomine Christi*, a tendency also adopted in several modern documents of the magisterium, for example, in *Presbyterorum ordinis*.[23] This tendency identifies the minister as an ambassador for Christ, representing Christ to the rest of the church. The vocabulary of *priesthood* when identified with ordained ministers tends to identify the ordained minister as someone representing Christ, Head of the Church, without whom the church may not pray. The identification of the priest as representing Christ eventually led to his assumption of the role of intermediary. Starting in the fifteenth century the bishops of Rome, for example, bore the title Pontifex Maximus, also used by the ancient Roman priesthood and the Roman emperors, indicating a "bridge builder" who mediates between the gods and humanity.[24] This contrasts with the original intent of ordination as the consecration of a minister to some kind

---

[23] Marliangeas, *Clés pour une théologie du ministère. Presbyterorum ordinis* also uses this language, as does Pope John Paul II's 1992 Apostolic Exhortation *Pastores dabo vobis*. Cf. David N. Power, "Representing Christ in Community and Sacrament," in *Being a Priest Today*, ed. Donald J. Goergen, OP (Collegeville, MN: Glazier, 1992), 97–123.

[24] Yves Congar, "Titres donnés au pape," *Concilium* (French edition), no. 108 (1975), 62–63. Quoted in Avery Dulles, *The Catholicity of the Church* (Oxford: Clarendon Press, 1985), 128.

of service.[25] In 2016 Vatican Secretary of State Cardinal Pietro Parolin explained how celibacy helps a priest grow in *persona Christi*:

> We can now refer to the two areas in which celibacy is closely connected: the identity of the priest [*prete*] inasmuch as he is configured to Christ and his pastoral mission. In fact, he not only performs individual acts *in persona Christi*, but is called to conform his whole life to the pastoral mission of the Master: living thus in the footsteps of Christ in a free, total and gratuitous offering for the People of God.[26]

Parolin continues that celibacy promotes a spousal relationship between the priest (here called alternately *presbitero* and *sacerdote*) and the church that allows the priest to give himself totally to the church. As Parolin notes, this theme is also present in John Paul II's Apostolic Exhortation *Pastores dabo vobis* (no. 29).[27]

The Apostolic Tradition instructs the bishop to distribute the "lots" or roles in the church community. Eventually, because of their sacerdotal status, presybters also distributed and legitimated roles or *klêroi*. By the middle of the third century, however, the *ordo* of clerics had monopolized all cultic and leadership ministries in the church. It was the duty of the

---

[25] See Fransen, "Orders and Ordination," 305–27; Yves Congar, "My Path-Findings in the Theology of Laity and Ministries," *The Jurist* 32 (1972): 180; idem, "Note sur une valeur des termes 'ordinare, ordinatio,'" *Revue des sciences religieuses* 58 (1984); Pierre van Beneden, *Aux origines d'une terminologie sacramentelle: Ordo, ordinare, ordinatio dans la littérature chrétienne avant 313*, Spicilegium sacrum Lovaniense, Études et documents, no. 38 (Louvain: Spicilegium sacrum Lovaniense, 1974); Macy, *The Hidden History of Women's Ordination*, 29–31.

[26] Cardinal Pietro Parolin, "Il cardinale Parolin al convegno sul celibato ecclesiastico–Il prete ordinato in persona Christi," *Osservatore Romano* (February 6, 2016).

[27] Ibid.

laity to support the clergy financially. Since women could not perform this duty, they were not laypeople until the middle of the fourth century.[28] With Constantine and the legalization of Christianity, the church began to borrow structures of the empire to organize itself. The eighth-century-forged "Donation of Constantine" attempted to legitimize the development of the hierarchy's civil as well as spiritual authority.

Gary Macy demonstrates that the eleventh to thirteenth centuries witnessed a significant change in the understanding of ordination in Christianity. Before the eleventh century the clergy were not the only people who were ordained to specific roles within the church. Ordination was not understood as conferring irrevocable power, nor did it involve a permanent commitment, even among the clergy. Macy believes that both women and men were ordained, and that some women were ordained to the clergy. We see this in the documents of the Council of Chalcedon in the fifth century, which refer to the ordination of women to the diaconate. The rituals of ordination described by the council explicitly allowed for the use of male or female pronouns. Macy concludes that there is no convincing reason, either linguistically or historically, to substantiate the proposal that the ordinations to orders, other than to the male presbyterate and diaconate, were simply blessings or commissionings, as some people propose. Orders or *ordines* were groups of people who performed the same ministry. Ordination incorporated someone into that group. It did not confer power; it recognized charism and authorized a person to exercise it.[29]

The sacerdotalization of the clergy was, alas, combined with a desire on the part of the clergy to assert power in the face of the nobility. This helped to shift the emphasis on the relation between the charism to perform a ministry and the power to

---

[28] Faivre, *Ordonner la fraternité*, 38.

[29] Macy, "The 'Invention' of Clergy and Laity in the Twelfth Century," 117–35; idem, *The Hidden History of Women's Ordination*; idem, "Diversity as Tradition: Why the Future of Christianity Is Looking More Like Its Past" (Santa Clara Lecture 14, Santa Clara University, Santa Clara, CA, November 8, 2007).

do so. As time went on, ordination didn't so much confirm and celebrate people's ministry because the community recognized that they had the talents to do them, but it conferred the power to do so as mediator of the divine. Only a priest had the power to change bread and wine into the body and blood of Christ, and that was because he received that power at ordination. Yet as late as the twelfth century some scholars claimed that the words of consecration, regardless of who pronounced them, effected that change.[30]

The Gregorian Reform begun in the eleventh century profoundly changed the theology and practice of ordination and ministry, putting into place the essentials of current Catholic theology. Under the influence of Gregory the Great, who was influenced by the fifth–sixth century Pseudo-Dionysius the Areopagite, the medieval church tended to identify earthly *ordines* with a divine hierarchy, infusing them with divine legitimacy. These eleventh-century reformers also reduced the number of *ordines* to two, presybter and diaconate, by claiming these were the only ones that Jesus himself had instituted. Many medieval scholars did not consider the episcopacy to be a separate *ordo* but part of the order of presbyter. In fact, the first official mention of bishops as being ordained to a distinct order is at the Second Vatican Council in the twentieth century. Macy asserts that the reduction of *ordines* to two thus eliminated the reality of ordination for many ministries that heretofore the church had considered to be real ordinations. The imposition of celibacy on the clergy by the Second Lateran Council in 1139 created a powerful clerical caste that alone enjoyed the recognition of ordination.

One of the first definitions of what became known as the sacrament of holy orders is found in the *Sentences* of Peter Lombard, composed between 1148 and 1151. Peter writes that the sacrament is "a certain sign, that is, something sacred, by

[30] See Macy, *The Hidden History of Women's Ordination*, 42. See also, idem, "Women and Priestly Ministry: The New Testament Evidence," *Catholic Biblical Quarterly* 41 (1979): 608–13.

which a spiritual power and office is given to the one ordained. Therefore a spiritual character is called an *ordo* or grade, where the promotion to power occurs."[31] Peter emphasized the gift of power imparted by ordination, with a resulting and perhaps unforeseen distinction between a person's God-given charism for the ministry and the right to do the ministry. In other words, persons with a gift for a ministry such as preaching could not exercise that gift until God gave them the power to do so through ordination.

Peter's understanding of sign or *signaculum* subsequently went through further evolution, eventually being equated with the sacramental character at baptism.[32] Thomas Aquinas used the same concept to express his belief that ordination need never be repeated, even if one left the ministry and then returned to it. Thomas, however, understood the character of ordination as descriptive rather than distinctive: ordination does not separate or distinguish the one ordained from everyone else but merely describes the person's new function in the Christian community.[33] The distinctive character of ordination is not in people but in the different ministries they do.

Gary Macy argues that the exclusion of women from ordination occurred during the Gregorian Reform.[34] He believes that women had been ordained before the twelfth century according to the definition of ordination in use at the time. Not all of those ordinations incorporated women into the clergy, but some either did or incorporated people into *ordines* that did the same ministries as the clergy. These included abbesses who were ordained and heard the confessions of their nuns, and deaconesses. He notes that early-twelfth-century scholars

---

[31] Peter Lombard, *Sentences*, Book 4, c. 14, PL 211: 1257b. Quoted in Macy, *The Hidden History of Women's Ordination*, 106.

[32] See Osborne, *Priesthood*, 105–6.

[33] See Schillebeeckx, "Theologische kanttekeningen bij de huidige priester-crisis," 402–34.

[34] Macy, *The Hidden History of Women's Ordination*; idem, "The 'Invention' of Clergy and Laity in the Twelfth Century"; idem, "Diversity as Tradition."

began to rely heavily on the commentary on the letters of Saint Paul by Ambrosiaster, whom they incorrectly identified as Ambrose of Milan. Confusing the two gave Ambrosiaster a lot more authority. Ambrosiaster argues that Romans and 1 Timothy demonstrate that Paul did not intend to include women in ministry. The canonist Rufinus, writing between 1157 and 1159, limited real ordination to ministry at the altar and relegated the ordinations of women to the category of a nonsacramental commissioning. Macy comments: "Rufinus's solution was ingenious. It carefully 'distinguished away' a thousand years' worth of reference to women's ordination." The imposition of celibacy on the clergy also tended to put women in a negative light, to put it mildly. Macy concludes: "The language of misogyny used to encourage and justify celibacy provides an important background for the exclusion of women from ordained ministry."[35]

Finally, we need to evaluate the argument that the ritual of ordination dates back to the New Testament and is the guarantee of apostolic succession or apostolicity. In 1947, Pope Pius XII, in his Apostolic Constitution *Sacramentum ordinis*, taught that the laying on of hands is the only matter necessary for ordination. The language that Catholic theology adopted after the Middle Ages used terms from Scholastic philosophy. Scholastic philosophy refers to the "schools" that developed during the Middle Ages, and is dominated by such figures as the Franciscan Saint Bonaventure and the Dominican Saint Thomas Aquinas. Scholastic theology describes sacraments as being composed of "matter" and "form" and of being instrumental causes of grace that work *ex opere operato*, that is, by performing the rite correctly.[36] The "matter" of the sacrament of holy orders in Scholastic terminology is the laying on of

---

[35] Macy, *The Hidden History of Women's Ordination*, 99, 114.

[36] See Council of Trent session 7, canons on the sacraments in general, in *Decrees of the Ecumenical Councils*, ed. Norman P. Tanner, 2 vols. (Washington, DC: Georgetown University Press, 1990), 2:684–85; and the Council of Florence Session 8, Bull of Union with the Armenians (November 22, 1439), pt. 5, in ibid., 1:540–50.

hands by the bishop and the "form" is some of the words of consecration. Although the gesture of the laying on of hands has a venerable history in the scriptures, where it signifies blessing and commissioning, its use as a formal rite can be identified with sufficient probability only to around 200 CE. Piet Fransen concludes, "It may therefore be presumed that the laying on of hands is not a 'substantial' element of the sacramental rite, but a rite instituted by the Church."[37] Edward Schillebeeckx demonstrates that historically in both the Eastern and Western churches the essential element of ordination was not the imposition of hands but a mandate to the one being ordained:

> Thus it emerges from the analysis of terms like *ordinatio, cheirotonia* and *cheirothesia* that the basic principle is that the minister of the church is one who is recognized as such by the whole of the church community (the people and its leaders), and is sent out to a particular community. . . . Outside this ecclesial context the liturgical laying on of hands is devoid of all meaning.[38]

It appears that although ordination needs some matter or material expression of mandate, it was not always the imposition of hands.

As we see, to speak of ordination in the New Testament and early church as we understand it today is really an anachronism. Conferring power, becoming another Christ, and monopolizing ministry in one class of people simply did not occur to people in the New Testament. That doesn't mean that the

---

[37] Fransen, "Orders and Ordination," 311.

[38] Schillebeeckx, *The Church with a Human Face*, 138–40. Schillebeeckx notes that *cheirotonia* does not denote "laying on of hands" but "appointing someone with the hand," while *cheirothesia* means "laying on of hands." See Eduard Lohse, "cheír" and "cheirotonéô," in *Theological Dictionary of the New Testament*, vol. 9, ed. Gerhard Kittel and Gerhard Friedrich, and trans. Geoffrey W. Bromiley (Grand Rapids, MI: Eerdmans, 1974), 424–37.

church cannot develop such a theology and forms of ministry if they work—when *work* means participating effectively in the great process of the universe's evolution, also known as salvation history. This theology and forms of ministry may have worked at one time, and may still work in some places, but their efficacy is showing signs of wear in many parts of the world. They have the significant drawback of devaluing the baptismal mission of all people and do not do a good job of recognizing and promoting the church's catholicity. There is no theological, historical, or scientific reason that prevents Christianity from changing them.[39]

The Distinction between Sacred and Secular Ministries

The post-Enlightenment redefinition of the concept of *religio* to *religion* separated reality into two spheres, as we have seen. The Enlightenment taught that science, which studied the immanent dimension of reality, was the only real way of knowing. Reality was limited to the immanent, and the meaning of the word *science* in English shifted from knowledge in general (from the Latin root *scire*) to knowledge attained by reason through empirical observation. Physics, chemistry, and biology are sciences; they provide real knowledge. Poetry is not science and, though it contemplates transcendence, does not provide real knowledge in Enlightenment thinking. The transcendent dimension of reality is known by belief, but the Enlightenment discounted the validity of that way of knowing. Although the Enlightenment could discount the human ability to know the transcendent dimension, it did recognize that many people have been and continue to be influenced by it. And thus was born a whole new discipline, that is, the academic study of religion,

---

[39] See Donald C. Maldari, SJ, "A Reconsideration of the Ministries of the Sacrament of Holy Orders," *Horizons* 34 (2007): 238–64.

in reality a branch of anthropology. Religious studies set out to examine the phenomena related to people's continued belief in the transcendent dimension of reality.

Religious studies got a boost from Émile Durkheim, the founder of sociology. Durkheim distinguished between what he called the sacred and the profane in religions:

> All known religious beliefs, whether simple or complex, present one common characteristic: they presuppose a classification of all the things, real and ideal, of which men think, into two classes or opposed groups, generally designated by two distinct terms which are translated well enough by the words *profane* and *sacred (profane, sacré)*. This division of the world into two domains, the one containing all that is sacred, the other all that is profane, is the distinctive trait of religious thought.[40]

The word *sacred* derives from the Latin word *sacrum*, which referred to something having to do with the gods and was associated with a temple and/or rituals. *Profane* derives from *profanum*, which referred to a place in front of a temple.[41] In Christian usage in the third century we find the difference between sacred and profane had acquired the sense of pure and impure.[42]

Unfortunately, Christian theologians and the church's magisterium have rather uncritically accepted the premise of the distinction between the sacred and the profane, often using the word *secular* as a synonym for *profane*. The general acceptance of this distinction has profoundly influenced the development

---

[40] Émile Durkheim, *The Elementary Forms of the Religious Life* (London: George, Allen and Unwin, 1915), 52ff. See further Mircea Eliade, *The Sacred and the Profane: The Nature of Religion* (New York: Harcourt Brace and World, 1959).

[41] Carsten Colpe, "The Sacred and the Profane," in *Encyclopedia of Religion*, ed. Lindsay Jones, 2nd ed., vol. 12 (Detroit: Macmillan Reference USA, 2005), 7964.

[42] Faivre, *Ordonner la fraternité*, 92–93.

of theology.[43] Current theology of ministry distinguishes between sacred and secular ministry, indicating that the latter is proper to the laity.[44] It isn't clear how the "secular clergy" fit in here; the concept *secular* is fraught with ambivalence.[45] English translations of the Vatican II documents *Lumen gentium*, *Apostolicam actuositatem,* and *Christifideles laici* often use it to translate the Latin words *mundus, profanus (LG 36)* and *saecularis.* A synonym for these words is *temporal (temporalis),* which *Apostolicam actuositatem* generously uses to describe the lay apostolate. In general the council preferred the word *apostolate* to describe what laypeople do and *ministry* for clerical activities. Perhaps the council's mind regarding the concept is succinctly expressed in *Lumen gentium,* which foresees the lay apostolate being "carried out in the ordinary surroundings of the world *(quod in communibus condicionibus saeculi*

---

[43] Raymonde Courtas and François A. Isambert, "La Notion de "sacré": Bibliographie thématique," *Archives de sciences sociales des religions* 22, no. 44.1 (July–September 1977): 119–38. The authors provide an extensive bibliography on the issue.

[44] See Timothy Fitzgerald, *Discourse on Civility and Barbarity: A Critical History of Religion and Related Categories* (Oxford: Oxford University Press, 2007), 71–108; Benedict Muellner, FSC, "Cullman: The Ambivalence of the Secular," *Continuum* 4 (Chicago, 1966): 76–91; Pope John Paul II, "A Vision of the Priest's Role," *Origins* 8 (February 15, 1979): 548–49; idem, *Christifideles laici* (December 30, 1988), 22; idem, *Message of John Paul II to Cardinal J. Francis Stafford on the Occasion of the Congress of the Catholic Laity* (November 21, 2000); Jean Galot, *Theology of the Priesthood* (San Francisco: Ignatius Press, 1985), 118.

[45] See T. A. Roberts, "The Sacred and the Secular in the Bible," *Modern Churchman* 1 (1957): 82–92; Mueller, "Cullmann: The Ambivalence of the Secular"; Ferdinand Klostermann, "Decree on the Apostolate of the Laity," *Commentary on the Documents of Vatican II,* vol. 3 (New York: Herder and Herder, 1967): 273–404; idem, "Constitution on the Church: Chapter 4: The Laity," in *Commentary on the Documents of Vatican II,* vol. 1 (New York: Herder and Herder, 1967): 231–52; Jean Beyer, "Secular Institutes," *Sacramentum Mundi* 6 (New York: Herder and Herder, 1970): 61–63; Ernest Niermann, "Secularization," *Sacramentum Mundi* 6 (New York: Herder and Herder, 1970): 64–71.

completur)" (LG 35). *Apostolicam actuositatem* elaborates on this theme: "Since the laity share in their own way in the mission of the church, their apostolic formation is specially characterized by the distinctively secular and particular quality of the lay state and by its own form of the spiritual life" (*AA* 20).

Avery Dulles opines that the council was aware of the ambiguity of the distinction between sacred ministry and profane/secular/temporal apostolate. The New Testament term *diakonia* describes most closely what we understand by ministry. Dulles writes that *diakonia* "embraces both official and unofficial activities dedicated to the upbuilding of the Christian community."[46] Many clergy engage in activities that are not "sacred," as understood by Durkheim, such as teaching, administration, social justice work, art, science, and so on. In 1972, Pope Paul VI established the offices of lector and acolyte as "lay ministries" in the *motu proprio Ministeria quaedam*. They sound suspiciously "sacred." Dulles also notes that the council had a difficult time defining exactly what the laity was.

The current understanding of the distinction among sacred, profane, religious, and secular assumes a cosmology that cannot account for the transcendent divine presence in evolving creation and introduces distinctions among various ministries that are artificial. It is also the product of the European Enlightenment thinking that is unique to Western culture. Thomas Fitzgerald thinks that it, along with the corresponding category of "religion," helped to support European imperialism in the nineteenth and twentieth centuries. Europeans considered peoples who did not distinguish between the sacred and profane to be primitive, backward, and uncivilized. Imagine: they still thought that God was actively present in all aspects of life, such as nature and their work! The same mentality prevents twenty-first-century Westerners from understanding the sensibility of Muslims, for whom Islam is not a "religion," as defined by the Enlightenment, but a culture by which they cultivate their

---

[46] Cardinal Avery Dulles, "Can Laity Properly Be Called 'Ministers'?" *Origins* 35 (April 20, 2006): 728.

humanity in function of their relationship with an all-present God. This sounds like what Christianity used to be.

Bruno Forte, theologian and currently archbishop of Chieti-Vasto in Italy, pleads for an outlook freed from the distinction between the sacred and the profane:

> Every worldly situation is susceptible to being lived in relation to the promise of faith, yet perceived and oriented from the "eschatological reserve," which is proper to the Christian. Separate spheres—sacred and profane, God and Caesar—from which each sphere would have its own specialists (sacred and lay ministers) do not exist; only the one sphere of existence exists, with the complexity of concrete relations of which it consists, in which Christians ought to situate themselves, according to their individual charism and ministry, with respect to the earthly reality ("rendering to Caesar that which is Caesar's") and in the permanent disturbing openness to the horizon of the kingdom ("and to God that which is God's").[47]

Avery Dulles agrees. "It would be a mistake, I believe, to make a sharp dichotomy between ministry in the church and apostolate in the world, as if it were necessary to choose between them."[48] All Christians have the right to cooperate with God in bringing creation to fulfillment, in promoting the *metánoia* by which people abandon and die to the legacy of sin, and use the energy of the Holy Spirit only to promote salvation history. Forte writes:

> *The entire local church proclaims the entire gospel to each and every person*: this affirmation means above all that mission is not directed to a profane space, different

---

[47] Bruno Forte, *Laicato e laicità, Saggi ecclesiologici*, 3rd ed. (Genoa: Marietti, 1987), 62–63. My translation.

[48] Dulles, "Can Laity Properly Be Called 'Ministers'?" 730.

from a sacred space. The frontier of evangelization is not a line of demarcation that is exteriorly recognizable between these spaces or between a worldly sphere and an ecclesiastical sphere, but is above all the place of saving decision in the heart of a person; it is the concrete situation in which the totality of an existence is decided for Christ and is attached to him.[49]

Evangelization is not simply a question of spreading the word about doctrine and belief. Evangelization is fundamentally the promotion of the good news of the kingdom. It is cooperating with God in everything that we are and do. It takes various forms of work in which people engage to put their charisms at the service of the energy that is the Holy Spirit for the growth of the kingdom. These are ministries. All contribute to the life of the community that is growing and evolving toward fulfillment. No one has charisms to do everything, but everyone has a charism to do something in this project. This is, indeed, the catholicity of ministry.

The Church's Hierarchical Structure

Piet Fransen, a *peritus* at Vatican II and professor at the Katholieke Universiteit in Leuven, Belgium, notes that churches in the first century developed governing bodies, called *presbuteroi* (elders) and later *episkopoi* (bishops), as we see in the Pastoral Epistles and the Acts of the Apostles. Although the New Testament speaks of these two ministries along with that of *diakonos* (deacon), they are never juxtaposed into something that we could call a hierarchy.[50] Avery Dulles writes, "Only in post-apostolic times did it become apparent that the unity and

---

[49] Forte, *Laicato e laicità*, 78. My translation.
[50] Piet Fransen, "Orders and Ordination," in *Sacramentum Mundi*, vol. 4 (New York: Herder and Herder, 1969); Günther Bornkamm, "*Diakonos*," in *Theological Dictionary of the New Testament*, vol. 6 (Grand Rapids, MI: Eerdmans, 1968), 667.

continuity of the Church as a whole required a body of leaders who would carry on the supervisory role originally performed by the apostles."[51] The arrangement slowly developed toward a monarchical structure in Asia Minor. Until perhaps the third century, Fransen thinks, the installation and "ordination" of bishops were done by the elders. Since this arrangement developed well after the time of Jesus and the apostolic community in the first century, Fransen concludes:

> This evidence does not permit us to affirm that the hierarchy of orders, i.e. monarchical bishop, college of elders and deacons, was a divine institution in the strict sense, or even an institution of the apostolic church, considered as a norm for later churches.[52]

Ignatius of Antioch emphasized that the office of the bishop included being the president of the liturgical assembly, underlining the bishop's role as leader. Tertullian was the first to refer to a bishop as *summus sacerdos*, that is, "high priest." As the church became more institutionalized, it tended to take over the structure of the Roman Empire.[53] The office of deacon developed from the Greek-speaking version of presbyter-bishop into what Ignatius thinks of as subordinates of bishops: "Thus deacons are to have in the church an honor similar to that of Christ; bishops to that of God."[54]

In the sixth century the church was thought of as the visible manifestation on earth of the kingdom in heaven. Thanks to the influence of Pseudo-Dionysius the Areopagite on Pope Gregory the Great, the order of the kingdom of heaven was revealed to be a hierarchy, and so was creation. The church, therefore, was necessarily—even ontologically—a sacred hierarchy, as Kenan Osborne explains:

---

[51] Dulles, *The Catholicity of the Church*, 118.
[52] Fransen, "Orders and Ordination," 310.
[53] Schillebeeckx, *The Church with a Human Face*, 132–33.
[54] H. W. Beyer, "*Diakonia*," in *Theological Dictionary of the New Testament* (Grand Rapids, MI: Eerdmans, 1968), 93.

Earthly hierarchies reflect divine hierarchies, but this implies that earthly hierarchies have the blessing, the endorsement, the power, to some degree, of the divine hierarchies. He (Pseudo-Dionysius) has three levels of reality: God, the angelic (or celestial) hierarchy, in descending order. . . . The ecclesiastical hierarchy (itself seen as being midway between the "legal" hierarchy of the Old Testament and the celestial hierarchy) consists again of three ranks of three: first the rank of the mysteries into which we are initiated . . . [baptism, eucharist, holy oil]; secondly the rank of those who perform the mysteries . . . [episkopoi, presbyters, deacons]; thirdly the rank of those who are being initiated . . . [monks, laity, and the catechumens/penitents].[55]

Gregory imagined the world as tripartite: clerics, monks, and laypeople. The emperor was in a class of his own, after the clerics. Because it mirrored heaven, this hierarchy was considered to be of divine origin. Peter Lombard went on to divide the clergy into seven orders to correspond to the seven gifts of the Holy Spirit, a division affirmed at the Council of Trent. Pseudo-Dionysius had opted for nine orders for the nine choirs of angels.[56]

During the Catholic Counter-Reformation, Robert Bellarmine defined the church as a "distinct society," which, of course, needed a structural organization. Thereafter the church began to understand itself explicitly as an "unequal and hierarchical society." The Council of Trent affirmed that the church is a hierarchy instituted by divine ordination, consisting of "bishops, priests, and ministers" (Canon 5 of the Decree on the Sacrament of Order). The First Vatican Council affirmed this teaching. A schema at that council, *Supremi Pastores*, reads: "No one is unaware that the church is a distinct society in which God has decreed that some are to command and

---

[55] Osborne, *Ministry*, 222.
[56] David N. Power, OMI, *Ministers of Christ and His Church: The Theology of the Priesthood* (London: Geoffrey Chapman, 1969), 115.

others to obey. These are seculars; the others are clerics" (no. 10).[57] Jesús Álvarez Gómez reports that the 1974 *Catechism* published by the Episcopal Commission for Education of the Spanish Episcopal Conference continues to teach this concept: "Not all Christians have the same dignity in the church, but by the will of Jesus Christ some teach and govern, and are the pastors, and others, under their authority, cooperate to realize the kingdom of God in the world, and these are the secular faithful" (question 155). Further: "The dignity of the priest is the greatest that there is on earth, because he is mediator between God and men" (question 533).[58]

Regardless of what the Spanish *Catechism* taught in 1974, in 1964 Vatican II assumed the existence of the hierarchy but, unlike the Council of Trent, it did not attribute a divine institution to it. It also put the chapter on the people of God in *Lumen gentium* before the one on the hierarchy. Bruno Forte, along with Fransen, opines that *Lumen gentium* intended to abolish a pyramid ecclesiology, in which grace trickles down from the hierarchy at the top to the laity at the bottom. They wished to replace this model with one of communion. Forte writes: "Ministries are situated as services in view of what the whole church ought to be and to do. The church, icon of the Trinity, is a mystery of Water, of Bread, of the Word and of the Spirit, and diversifies in the richness of gifts and of services of which it is full." Forte sees a greater emphasis on the pneumatological, that is, spiritual, aspect of the church, shifting the model of church from hierarchy to communion: "The Spirit is seen to act in the whole community, to make it the body of Christ, kindling in it the multiplicity of charisms which then are configured in the variety of ministries to the service of the growth of the community itself."[59]

---

[57] In Spanish, Jesús Álvarez Gómez, "La orden y el laicado," 428. English translation mine.

[58] Ibid., 429. English translation mine.

[59] Bruno Forte, *La chiesa icona della Trinità: Breve ecclesiologia,* Universale teologica 9 (Brescia: Queriniana, 1984), 33. English translation mine.

An emphasis on the action of the Holy Spirit does not automatically mean that the hierarchical structure of the church cannot foster the kindling of catholic ministries for the good of the growth of the community. In many ways this structure has worked well over the centuries. The catholic *religio* was the means of the cultivation of rich civilizations from Ireland to India for centuries and made important contributions to civilizations spread throughout the world after the sixteenth century. The positive fruits of the *religio*, organized as a hierarchy, are undeniable. By these fruits we can judge that God was able to work through that *religio* in its hierarchically organized form. Through the hierarchically structured church the Holy Spirit was able to energize the church, inspire ministry, and promote the world's evolution in its growth as the body of Christ. The hierarchy served in the capacity as leaders. That some of those leaders did not and do not cooperate with the Holy Spirit does not result in an indictment of the whole system. The basis of judging the system's validity is its usefulness. Does it work? Is it successful in promoting evolution?

Some theologians, such as Matthew Levering, continue to hold "that the Father, Son, and Holy Spirit willed a hierarchical church, notwithstanding the inevitable sinfulness of the members of the hierarchical priesthood, because of the theocentric pattern of gifting and receptivity that hierarchy fosters in the Church."[60] Levering proposes that God sends the Holy Spirit into the church to animate it according to the pattern of the Trinity, which he understands as hierarchical communion: "Precisely by configuring the believer to the analogous gifting and receptivity constitutive of the Persons of the Father, Son, and Holy Spirit, hierarchy belongs to the salvific accomplishment of the unity that befits the church."[61] Levering understands the power of salvation as being distributed through the hierarchy.

---

[60] Matthew Levering, *Christ and the Catholic Priesthood: Ecclesial Hierarchy and the Pattern of the Trinity* (Chicago: Hillenbrand Books, 2010), 10. See also Galot, *Theology of the Priesthood*, 77–86.

[61] Levering, *Christ and the Catholic Priesthood*, 52.

He makes this assertion first by peering into what theologians call the immanent model of the Holy Trinity. The immanent model is our human attempt to understand who God is and how God is within the Godhead itself. This is the equivalent of saying, "God is x, y, and z." The only way people can make any such affirmations of who God is, is through divine revelation. God tells us who and how God is. And the only means of revelation is our experience of God and how God works in creation. The way God works in creation is called the economic model of the Trinity. This name comes from the Greek word for the management of a household: *oikonomia*. Theologians know that we need to be extremely careful when speaking of who and how God is. God is infinite, but our ability to understand God is not. All of our descriptions of God are filtered through our experience and our limited ability to understand anything, including God. This is why theology has developed what are called cataphatic and apophatic branches. Cataphatic theology offers positive descriptions of who God is but always must qualify those descriptions by admitting that they fall short of God's reality. Apophatic theology offers negative descriptions, that is, it makes statements of who God is *not,* precisely because God exceeds all our ability to describe God.

Levering's assertion that the hierarchy mirrors how the Trinity, which is a hierarchy, is, is a cataphatic statement. It needs to be put into the context of how we know who the Trinity is and what images we use to describe God. As we saw, the development of the hierarchy in the church occurred as the church adapted to its environment and adopted the organizational structures of the Roman Empire and, later, feudal society. Christians experienced God in that organizational structure and projected that organizational structure back onto God. God didn't so much make the church into hierarchy as the church made God into a hierarchy! Theologians described God in terms of what they knew but also humbly admitted that God goes beyond all our descriptions. So, is God a hierarchy? Yes and no.

Another aspect of our limited ability to know who and how God is, is in our understanding of God as unchanging but ever changing at the same time. The sixth-century-BCE Greek philosopher Heraclitus knew, well before modern physics, that "everything changes and nothing stands still." Christian theology reflects upon who and how God is in light of Heraclitus's insight by speaking about the divine *perichoresis* or *circumincessio* to describe the intimate relationship among the three persons of the Trinity. Jürgen Moltmann understands this word to describe the three persons engaged in an eternal dance that emphasizes mutuality rather than lordship, God who is egalitarian rather than hierarchical.[62] This mutuality in turn is reflected in the dynamic structure of creation.

In light of the thought of Moltmann and many other modern theologians, how do we evaluate Levering's proposal? Is the church a hierarchy because God is? Yes and no. It can be, but it doesn't have to be. What the church has to be is the effective way of promoting salvation history. It has to be the community of persons who together are animated by the Holy Spirit in order to grow into eternal communion through Christ's death and resurrection. It has to be the open system that processes energy in the universe, becoming ever more complex as it is propelled toward and beyond entropy. In all this the church must be catholic, including in offering all of its members the possibility to exercise their charisms as expressions of the Holy Spirit. If a hierarchical structure does that best, then let the church be organized as a hierarchy. The only criterion for

---

[62] Jürgen Moltmann, *Experiences of Theology: Ways and Forms of Christian Theology*, trans. Margaret Kohl (Minneapolis: Fortress Press, 2000), 318–19. See Stanley J. Grenz, *Rediscovering the Triune God: The Trinity in Contemporary Theology* (Minneapolis: Fortress Press, 2004); Elizabeth A. Johnson, "Trinity: To Let the Symbol Sing Again," *Theology Today* 54 (1997): 298–311; Leonardo Boff, *Trinity and Society*, trans. Paul Burns (Maryknoll, NY: Orbis Books, 1988); Denis Edwards, *The God of Evolution: A Trinitarian Theology* (New York: Paulist Press, 1999); Jack Mahoney, SJ, "Evolution, Altruism, and the Image of God," *Theological Studies* 71 (2010): 677–701.

how the church organizes itself, however, is not conformation to a cataphatic and therefore unavoidably flawed understanding of God. It is based upon the law of natural selection: what works. What works in one part of the globe may not work in another. Some cultures are hierarchically organized, and they successfully promote people's cultivation. Others, as in the West, used to be hierarchically organized but are no longer. If hierarchy is not effective in those cultures, the church has a right to reorganize itself, so long as it remains true to the faith passed down to us from the apostles.

Chapter 5

Catholic Ministry at the Service of the Church

On March 19, 2016, Pope Francis published a letter written to Cardinal Marc Ouellet, PSS, president of the Pontifical Commission for Latin America, after meeting with the participants of the Commission for Latin America and the Caribbean. The letter elaborates on the pope's understanding of the church as the people of God and how those people ought to interact and work together. He cuts to the quick early on in the short document. He expresses frustration with pious platitudes that call for updating and change but don't seem to do anything. He writes: "I now recall the famous phrase: 'the hour of the laity has come,' but it seems the clock has stopped."

The pope attributes at least some of the difficulty to clericalism and the frustration of the laity in exercising their baptismal life. He calls on the clergy to be good pastors—a theme near and dear to Francis's heart. He frequently encourages the clergy to be so close to the people that they will be "shepherds living with the smell of the sheep."[1] Francis warns:

> Often we have given in to the temptation of thinking that committed lay people are those dedicated to the works

---

[1] Pope Francis, speaking at Holy Thursday Chrism Mass, reported in *The Catholic Telegraph* (March 28, 2013); see also Diego Fares, *Il profumo del pastore* (Milan: Ancora, 2015).

of the Church and/or the matters of the parish or the
diocese, and we have reflected little on how to accompany
baptized people in their public and daily life; on how in
their daily activities, with the responsibilities they have,
they are committed as Christians in public life.[2]

The pope proposes that "lay people need new forms of organization and of celebration of the faith. . . . As St. Ignatius would
say, 'in line with the necessities of place, time and person.' In
other words, not uniformly."[3] He calls for inculturation that is
more akin to the work of artisans than factories. His outlook
is a powerful expression of the church's catholicity: one size
does not fit all. Right forms of ministry must be crafted for real
places, times, and persons. Those forms need to facilitate the
life of all the baptized, the entire people of God, as all respond
to the divine vocation to be co-creators of the kingdom of God.

The church, the people of God, both is and is becoming one,
holy, catholic, and apostolic. It is these characteristics because
it is "of God," the body of Christ, the realization of salvation
history. It is becoming these characteristics because salvation
history is completed only inchoately. We live in eschatological
tension; the kingdom is here and is coming. In light of our
consideration of data from the natural and social sciences, and
our reflection upon ministry in scripture and tradition, let us
consider how catholic ministry can not only repair the stopped
clock to which the pope referred, but even "advance the hour,"
as Jesus's mother asked him at the marriage feast of Cana.

One

The natural sciences give us an awe-inspiring—perhaps even
awesome—picture of the universe as one. The entire known

---

[2] Pope Francis, "Letter of His Holiness Pope Francis to Cardinal
Marc Ouellet."
[3] Ibid.

universe has a common origin, the Big Bang. Everything in it is somehow connected to everything else. Everything that happens affects the whole, however slightly. The laws of thermodynamics are equally applicable in the two trillion galaxies that scientists estimate exist (at last count in 2017). Theology expresses our faith that the universe is the creation of God—or perhaps one of God's creations. Maybe God is creating other universes that we don't know about. In any case, we believe that God is creating this one, and with Teilhard we recognize it as the divine milieu. God's presence permeates it. There is no place where God is not. Nothing happens except by divine energy. What we call evil is the conscious frustration of God's will by abusing that energy.

The laws of thermodynamics confirm Teilhard's vision that the whole universe is converging. For physics, this is occurring through the distribution of energy released at the Big Bang. As we have seen, as energy is distributed it forms matter, and it organizes matter into increasingly complex open systems that serve to distribute energy ever more efficiently through the universe. That energy fires all matter in the universe to become more and more complex and organized, culminating in what we generally call life. Life is really the most complex open system of matter that we know. We do know that there is a great deal in the universe that we don't know. Since we don't know what we don't know, it's hard to estimate how much we don't know—but discoveries of things like dark matter and energy, black holes, and so on should keep our minds busy for a few millennia. Theological reflection on the increased complexity of matter under the influence of energy points to the increased development of the incarnation of the Son through the Holy Spirit. Through faith we gaze upon the work of the Holy Trinity in the universe—the economic model of the Trinity—and affirm that the Father creates through the Son by the power of the Holy Spirit. The Son, though greater than the universe, permeates it and, for reasons best known to God, develops with it. We believe that the fullness of the Son's presence in the universe occurred in Jesus Christ. In and through him creation comes to completion and fulfillment.

Another aspect of the laws of thermodynamics is entropy. As energy becomes and organizes matter with its resulting distribution, there is less energy in the universe. Energy and matter, recall, are two forms of the same stuff. In effect, energy is propelling us toward increased complexity and organization while at the same time leaving behind a trail of decreased complexity and organization. When all energy is equally distributed, all complexity and organization will cease, culminating in what we generally call death.

Theological refection on Christ's life, death, and resurrection helps us to find meaning in the physical processes we observe in the universe. Jesus's whole life was about bringing people together by the power of the Holy Spirit. His gathering of all his disciples, each with different charisms and ministries, illustrates the salvation history we see playing out in physics. His death, experienced symbolically in his baptism as well as in the Eucharist, and then physically in his crucifixion, expresses the entropy that leads to death. His resurrection and ascension by the power of God are the ways by which his body, the church, transcends the death of the universe to journey into the great unknown of the universe's new life in union with God.

A consideration of data and theories from the social sciences closer to home reveals how everything on earth changes according to the Darwinian theory of evolution. Through natural selection traits develop that serve to promote survival. Among those basic traits are tendencies toward competition and cooperation, selfishness and altruism. Both have been essential for survival in everything from atoms to ecosystems. We humans have inherited both instincts. The development of our consciousness has moved us into biocultural evolution at a level unknown to other species. We are now able to direct nature to a far greater degree than any other creature on the planet. Along with this increased consciousness we have developed conscience, which gives us indications of what constitutes success in survival that transcends the immanent dimension of reality. Conscience informs people, regardless of specific cultures, that there is something wrong with selfishness and something admirable in altruism. Successful human culture in general is guided by this perception and attempts to cultivate humanity toward this objective good.

Christian theology reflects on these data from the natural and social sciences. It sees the pull to move beyond selfishness and the admiration for altruism as inspired by divine revelation. Through faith we perceive not only the economic model of the Trinity but the immanent one. God is community—not just *a* community, but community itself. The three persons of the divine Community live in and from altruism, otherwise known as love. We humans feel called by God to participate in community. As the First Letter of John enigmatically describes our present and future: "Beloved, we are God's children now; what we will be has not yet been revealed. What we do know is this: when he is revealed, we will be like him, for we will see him as he is" (1 John 3:2). In other words, we are now the children of God evolving toward being ever more like God—a state which goes beyond our ability to imagine. We do not yet know what it is to be like God, but whatever it is, we will be one as the Father and the Son are one (John 17:21–23).

In the meantime we have to deal with that pesky inherited selfishness that separates us. We need grace, gifts of the Holy Spirit, to transform us, to effect the *metánoia* of baptism, by which we die to selfishness and are reborn into one community of love. One manifestation of selfishness is competition, a trait that has served us well in natural selection and which has such a strong hold on us that we almost universally ignore its negative consequences. There must always be an *other* in competition, someone or something that doesn't belong, is not part of the One. When no *other* is on the horizon, we invent one. This is how competitive games work. They are negative sacraments of selfishness, with deep roots in our evolutionary fabric.

The natural sciences tell us that selfishness, and its manifestation in cooperation, is also deeply rooted in our evolutionary fabric. Remember that one of the main, though not the only, reasons we cooperate with one another is to form groups that compete more successfully against other people. It, too, is a trait that favors survival in natural selection. Cooperation, too, is an inherited instinct, even if it is usually tainted by selfishness. The energy that brings matter together works most effectively when all components of the open system work cooperatively. Theological reflection points to imitating, participating in the oneness of the Trinity. The three persons of the Trinity cooperate absolutely, without a hint of selfishness or competition. This may strike people as infinitely boring. We are energized by the competition that brings people together to cooperate against a common foe—witness the popularity of the World Cup, the Super Bowl, the World Series, and so on. We have the impression that a lack of competition leads to stagnation. Faith, however, calls us to abandon the selfishness that motivates us to cooperate in order to compete more effectively. Faith calls us to a dynamic, universal cooperation that imitates, indeed, participates, in the dynamic life of the Trinity. The theory of *perichoresis* that faith proposes, however, guarantees eternal dynamism in unchangeable changing unity.

The church, a sacrament of the unity that Christ effected, must craft ways to allow and to promote all members of the church to work to promote creation's evolution toward unity. Just as Christ brought all disciples together and empowered them to use their charisms, so must the church. Any fundamental division among classes of church members inhibits that cooperative, unified effort. As Saint Paul astutely notes, and anyone with eyes can observe, no one can do everything well. Paul further teaches that no job is more honorable than any other. Leadership theories these days solve that problem by telling us that everyone is a leader. That strikes me as flawed. Not everyone has the charism for leadership without changing the definition of leadership. It is also at times a ploy with a subtext that reads, "Some are more leaders than others." The church is the unified body of Christ. All members should be able to express themselves through the exercise of charisms that are gifts of God for the building up of the one church and each of its members. Not all are leaders. But the charism of leadership is useful only to organize and coordinate the universal cooperation of the one church. Leaders enable all to exercise their right to ministry according to their charisms.

Finally, the post-Enlightenment redefinition of *religio* as *religion*, which is an optional and suspect sphere of reality distinct from public life, along with sociology's introduction of a distinction between sacred and profane or secular, is artificial and deleterious. It introduces division within the church such that at its best the church proposes to dialogue with the world—as if it were an entity apart. It considers some ministries to be religious and sacred and others to be secular and profane. This leaves one with the probably unwanted impression that some ministries, categorized as secular, either do not really contribute to the life of the body of Christ, to the Christian culture or *religio*, or to the advancement of salvation history, or do so only peripherally. Sacred ministries are thought of as belonging to a higher category. All ministries are equal in the body of Christ, but some are more equal than others. Yet cannot plumbing, teaching, carpentry, construction, medicine, economics, law enforcement, firefighting, and the practice of law all be ways for people to use their charisms expressly for the life of the community? Can we not call them ministries in the Christian *religio*, that is, works that cooperate with God in creation?

Holy

The pedigree of our English word *holy* can be traced back to the Proto-Indo-European word *kailo-*, meaning whole. Through history the word also developed into *health*. Holy, whole, and health thus all have the same origin, and their meanings today are related. In the natural and social sciences *whole* and *healthy* describe systems that are working well. They are systems that are efficiently degrading energy, that is, distributing it evenly. This is what they are supposed to do, and they're doing it well.

They are systems that are surviving through natural selection, adapting as necessary to changing conditions. Part of that success is due to the contributions of each element in the system.

When we describe the church as holy, we imply that it is doing what it is supposed to do. It lives from the energy in the universe that is the presence of the Holy Spirit. It nourishes all members of the body of Christ by distributing that energy so that each member can live, that is, use that energy to express himself or herself and sustain the one church. The church is holy because God is holy, and God permeates the church.

The Bible in various ways describes God as holy.[4] God is perfect and complete, being and doing what God is supposed to do. The most common way that the Old Testament describes what God is supposed to do is to be kind and merciful; the New Testament translates those characteristics as love. Matthew 5:48 describes God as perfect, fulfilled, without blemish, complete *(téleios)*. Luke's version of the same line, 6:36, describes God as merciful or compassionate *(oiktírmon)*. Both Gospels tell us to be like God: perfect and merciful. The Old Testament says the same thing: some version of "be holy, for I the LORD your God am holy" (Lev 11:44–45; 19:2; 20:26; 21:8). First Peter 15—16 quotes this idea and applies it to the readers of the epistle. These texts give the same message: being perfect means being merciful and compassionate and vice versa.

The First Letter of John elaborates on God's holiness and how we become holy like God is. The letter describes God's holiness as love and exhorts us to live like God:

> Little children, you are from God, and have conquered them [spirits of the anti-Christ]; for the one who is in you is greater than the one who is in the world. . . . Beloved, let us love one another, because love is from God; everyone who loves is born of God and knows God.

---

[4] See "*Qadosh*," in *Theological Dictionary of the Old Testament*, vol. 12 (Grand Rapids, MI: Eerdmans, 2012), 521–45.

Whoever does not love does not know God, for God is love. (1 John 4:4–8)

It is precisely by living love, by putting love into action, that people grow in holiness and out of sin.

Ministry is so many ways that people can put their love into action in the world. The result of that action is the holiness of each person and the whole community. As Pope Francis writes in the Apostolic Exhortation *Gaudete et exultate*: "Do you work for a living? Be holy by laboring with integrity and skill in the service of your brothers and sisters" (*GE* 14). Ministry is one of the ways that people cooperate with God in the process of bringing evolution to wholeness, of fulfilling salvation history. Philip Hefner writes:

> In the Christian version of the myth [of Adam and Eve], human nature is joined with God's gracious energy for the fulfillment of God's intentions, and it requires lives of self-giving love, even to the point of death. This is what the figure of Jesus Christ communicates.[5]

The church sanctifies, makes its members holy, by providing opportunities to let the divine energy flow through them. Since God permeates every nook and cranny of the universe, the entire universe is called to be holy. It is, as Teilhard called it, the divine milieu. All human acts done in love promote the evolution of the universe's holiness and, curiously, the glory of God. Scripture describes these acts as service, the word we translate as ministry. The application of Occam's Razor does away with the need for a distinction between sacred and secular service or ministry. The reality is that all service done in love contributes to the church's holiness and serves to promote salvation history as a whole. Mary Elsbernd's study shows that people

---

[5] Philip Hefner, "The Animal That Aspires to Be an Angel," *Dialog: A Journal of Theology* 48 (2009): 165.

have a desire to serve. They feel a vocation to serve.[6] Her study was done within the context of the traditional distinction of sacred and secular ministries in a school of theology, which no doubt influenced and perhaps even limited the descriptions of the kinds of ministries to which people felt called. For the most part, those people felt called to what has been described as the participation of the laity in priestly ministry. A change in perspective that results in calling the various services people do for the good of the community ministry would clarify to both those people and the whole community that their work is a direct ministry, not a participation in someone else's. Furthermore, such a change in perspective would clarify and emphasize to people who do service now classified as secular that what they do contributes directly to the promotion of the holiness of members of the church.

The advantage of clarifying and emphasizing the salvific nature of all service is that it helps all people better to understand the character of that service. A better understanding is beneficial to how we manage and direct our biocultural evolution. It sheds light on the real purpose of all work—manual labor, social services, education, manufacturing, business, and so on. Knowing the real purpose of all those forms of work helps people to discern how they ought to be expressions of love, and thus how to do them such that they are expressions of love. This understanding and knowledge are useful both for those engaged in those works as well as the leaders of the community whose ministry is to coordinate and promote the ministries of all members of the community. When works are understood as ministries each individual and the whole community can consciously direct them as integral parts of the *religio*, the culture that promotes holiness.

---

[6] Mary Elsbernd, OSF, "Listening to a Life's Work: Contemporary Callings to Ministry," in *Revisiting the Idea of Vocation: Theological Explorations*, ed. John C. Haughey, SJ (Washington, DC: Catholic University of America Press, 2004), 196–219.

Teilhard called for the recognition of the salvific value of every service or ministry when he writes of the "divinization of our activities" in the *Divine Milieu*. Teilhard ponders the value of human activity done "in the name of Jesus Christ." He muses: "Moreover, the very expansion of our energy (which reveals the core of our autonomous personality) is, ultimately, only our obedience to a will to be and to grow, of which we can master neither the varying intensity nor the countless modes."[7] He goes on to plead for an appreciation of the salvific value of human work. The economy of salvation, which he also calls our "divinization," can be understood in the following way:

> At the heart of the universe, each soul exists for God, in our Lord. But all reality, even material reality, around each one of us, exists for our souls. Hence, all sensible reality, around each one of us, exists, through our souls, for God in our Lord.[8]

God calls, embraces, and gives life to everything. Everything that exists is for the good of our growing in our relationship with God. Through creation we are nourished by "the innumerable energies of the tangible world." We grow together in holiness through our interaction with creation: "With each one of our works, we labor—in individual separation, but no less really—to build the Pleroma; that is to say, we bring to Christ a little fulfilment. . . . Each one of our works, by its more or less remote or direct effect upon the spiritual world, helps to make perfect Christ in his mystical totality."[9] Although work appears simply to be a way of "earning our daily bread," its real worth is much greater: "But its essential virtue is on a higher level: through it we complete in ourselves the subject of the divine union; and through it again we somehow make

---

[7] Pierre Teilhard de Chardin, The Divine Milieu (New York: Harper Torchbooks, 1965), 49.

[8] Ibid., 56.

[9] Ibid., 62.

to grow in stature the divine term of the one with whom we are united, our Lord Jesus Christ."[10] Thanks to the incarnation, "nothing is profane." All work, energized by the power of love, that is the Holy Spirit, serves to sanctify the world. Thinking in terms of various groups in the church whose members "bind themselves to such and such virtue in particular," such as mercy, poverty, missions, and so on, Teilhard wonders why there cannot also be:

> Why should there not be men vowed to the task of exemplifying, by their lives, the general sanctification of human endeavor?—men whose common religious ideal would be to give a full and conscious explanation of the divine possibilities or demands which any worldly occupation implies—men, in a word, who would devote themselves, in the fields of thought, art, industry, commerce and politics, etc., to carrying out in the sublime spirit these demands—the basic tasks which form the very bonework of human society?[11]

Too often, he continues, these are left to unbelievers, but they too, consciously or not, contribute to building the kingdom of God because their work is animated by the Holy Spirit, the divine energy. Recognizing the salvific nature of all work "bestows significance and beauty and a new lightness on what we are already doing."[12]

Teilhard's thought springs from his Jesuit soul, formed by the *Spiritual Exercises* of Saint Ignatius. He values all human work not in a Pelagian effort to earn salvation, to build the kingdom of God without divine help. His musings are inspired by the second week of the *Exercises* in which the exercitant grows in intimate friendship with Christ, the "knowledge" of Christ that is the means of joining Christ. The exercitant

---

[10] Ibid., 63.

[11] Ibid., 67.

[12] Ibid., 70.

begins the second week by accepting the invitation of Jesus, the eternal king, to labor along with him for the salvation of the world. That labor will find its denouement in the third and fourth weeks of the exercises, through Jesus's passion and death that leads to his resurrection. Thus, after Teilhard emphasizes the value of human work in *The Divine Milieu*, he goes on to meditate on the "divinization of our passivities." These will serve to render us ever more open to being led through and beyond our efforts to the fulfillment of salvation history in our own death and resurrection.

Catholic

The church's catholicity is essentially a participation in the catholicity of the universe. As we have discussed, the universe is nearly infinitely diverse. It consists of a mindboggling number of different kinds of units, from subatomic to galactic. On top of that these units interact with one another in such a plethora of ways that by the time we have described some interactions, they've already changed. Some we cannot see but know they are there only by their effects. And there are effects for whose causes we don't have any explanations—at least not yet. The universe is like a vast symphonic orchestra, with different instruments playing a variety of notes simultaneously.

Closer to home, our planet teams with diverse systems that complement one another through cooperation and competition in changing environments. Diversity and adaptability are essential for survival. Systems and species that become too specialized cannot adapt to changing environments and are transformed into something quite different. When we say that they become extinct, we mean that their configuration of matter fades away and is absorbed into other, different configurations in order to continue to distribute energy. The more diverse and flexible systems are, the greater their chances for survival. Whether we like it or not, roaches can live just about anywhere.

We took a look at how the church has understood its catholicity in the tradition in Chapter 3. The church participates in the diversity and flexibility of the universe. Diversity and flexibility are characteristics of how the universe evolves and thus how the church, the body of Christ, participates in salvation history. The church's diversity and flexibility are essential characteristics of its catholicity. It is through this diversity and flexibility, this catholicity, that the Father, through the Son, by the power of the Holy Spirit, moves creation toward its fulfillment. The catholicity that characterizes the universe, the evolving body of the Son that crescendos in Jesus, reveals the catholicity of the Triune God (Col 1:15–17). Avery Dulles writes: "If Christ is the universal principle of creation and redemption, he has, so to speak, a cosmic catholicity. In his incarnate existence he is, under God, the concrete universal."[13] Both the immanent and economic Trinity are catholic. God works salvation in a catholic way. For human biocultural evolution to be successful, we, too, should work in a catholic way.

Avery Dulles summarizes the modern way of understanding catholicity from Vatican II:

> In summary, Vatican II presents catholicity not as a monotonous repetition of identical elements but rather as reconciled diversity. It is a unity among individuals and groups who retain their distinctive characteristics, who enjoy different spiritual gifts, and are by that very diversity better equipped to serve one another and thus advance the common good. Individual Christians and local churches are bound to one another in mutual service and mutual receptivity. This relationship is founded not upon domination but on a free exchange of trust and respect.[14]

Catholicity replaces the competition that divides people with cooperation that unites. Members of the community use their

---

[13] Avery Dulles, SJ, *The Catholicity of the Church* (Oxford: Clarendon Press, 1985), 39; see also 44.

[14] Ibid., 24.

different gifts for the common good. Dulles calls catholicity both "a divine gift and a human task."[15] The "divine gift" is the revelation of how God is. In our limited ability to know God we describe God as a community of three persons, each of whom contributes something different to the life of the divine Community. Speaking analogously we might say that each divine person has different charisms that flow from the unity of the Trinity and animate it. Each, again analogously, works, contributing something different that enriches the whole. God's self-revelation indicates to us our task to abandon our individualism and selfishness, our instinct to compete, and instead to work cooperatively. Catholicity complements unity by emphasizing the value of the contributions of each member of the community.

Dulles alludes to Irenaeus by describing the church's catholicity as "a participation in Christ's dynamic power to recapitulate both humanity and the cosmos under his universal headship."[16] Irenaeus developed his theory of recapitulation in his controversy with the Gnostics, who divided the world into physical and spiritual parts, with little use for the physical. Irenaeus answered that Christ brings the entire creation into one body with Christ as the body's head. People's service understood in the light of catholicity recognizes that every one of them, however mundane or physical, is essential to the process of recapitulation.

The flexibility that characterizes success in evolution is also a characteristic of catholicity. The Catholic Church has at times lost sight of this truth, as Avery Dulles points out: "Just as in early modern times Catholics tended to confuse universality with uniformity, so they tended to equate continuity with immutability."[17] Different and changing times require different and changing ways of engaging in biocultural evolution. The Christian *religio* must adapt to the times by expressing the

---

[15] Ibid., 27.
[16] Ibid., 43.
[17] Ibid., 99.

same faith in different ways. The work in which people engage has clearly changed over the centuries. Think how hard it is these days to find a butcher, a baker, or a candlestick maker. In Western societies it is not uncommon for people to change careers every so often depending on changing circumstances, the discovery of hidden talents, or the discovery that they didn't have the talents they thought they had. The requirement of a permanent commitment to a particular ministry seems unnecessary and, in light of the flexibility characteristic of catholicity, perhaps even unwise. The church's catholicity would be better served if, after serious discernment, people were able to change the type of service they contribute to the community. There is no reason why a person who undertakes a new type of service could not return to the first if circumstances suggest that would be wise. The outlook of leaving behind yet being able to resume a former ministry preserves the wisdom of the theology of sacramental character of ordination without imposing unnecessary restrictions.

The catholicity of the church springs from its genesis in creation. Like everything else in the universe, it evolves following the laws of nature, changing and adapting. Because it is the body of Christ it responds to the divine vocation to be animated by the Holy Spirit to promote holiness. Scientists tell us that no operation, no change, no adaptation, no form in nature can be attributed to something outside of the universe. Theologians must acknowledge that God does not manipulate nature. God does not impose anything on salvation history. Rather, God continually calls and animates, leaving how history develops up to the laws of nature that God created. The position that God intended the church to organize itself in a particular way at any time, much less forever, seems untenable. As we have seen, the organizational structure of the church has varied throughout history, even if we look at that history only starting from the first century CE. Avery Dulles recognizes this principle when, referring to Karl Rahner, he states that Vatican II "exhibited a consciousness of cultural pluralism."[18] The hierarchical structure of the Catholic Church developed within the context of the Mediterranean world and Europe. It grew from the bottom up—not because it was dictated by Jesus, but because it worked. The church in those areas allowed, respected, and even rejoiced in the diversity of forms by which Christians expressed their faith, especially in the liturgy. That diversity was effective. It existed consonant with the catholicity of the world. It was supportive of the biocultural evolution by which people worked as co-creators with God. The catholicity of forms helped, and continues to help the church to be a sacrament of salvation. It appeals to humanity in our diversity and invites full participation of all, in the spirit of Saint Paul's image of the church as a body in 1 Corinthians 12 and Ephesians 4. If a hierarchical structure of ministry is conducive to the church's catholicity, if it serves to stimulate all members of the community to participate in and contribute to the common good; if it supports and encourages all members to recognize that their service done in love promotes salvation history, then that structure is serving its purpose. If that is not the case, consideration should be given to revising the organizational structure better to express the church's catholicity. This principle seems to express the thought of Vatican II when it taught:

> Likewise the Church, living in various circumstances in the course of time, has used the discoveries of different cultures so that in her preaching she might spread and explain the message of Christ to all nations, that she might examine it and more deeply understand it, that she might give it better expression in liturgical celebration and in the varied life of the community of the faithful. (*GS* 58)

In addition to the hierarchy in general, consideration of the distinction between the clergy and laity is useful to determine

---

[18] Ibid., 75.

the role it plays in fostering catholicity in the church. The critique of the distinction that we did in the previous chapter suggests that for the most part it does not. Indeed, the distinction may play a major role in why the hour of the laity has not yet come. The distinction as explained in Vatican II documents does not express well Teilhard's vision of the divinization of our activities. The problem with dividing people into clergy and laity for the catholicity of the church is that the division assumes that each member of the clergy has a vast array of charisms that laypeople either do not have or cannot exercise. It imposes an artificial distinction that does not accurately reflect people's charisms. Ministries reserved to the clergy require charisms for public speaking, spiritual counseling, pastoral care of the sick, teaching, parish administration, leadership, organizing people and projects, relating to youth, and others. Few individuals can do all those things well. There are laypeople who do have those charisms, but because they are not members of the clergy, they are not permitted to use them directly. Even when they do exercise them by participating in the ministry of the clergy, they can never be the minister of any of the sacraments except matrimony—and not even that in the Orthodox Church. Magisterial documents foresee the services that the laity perform as focused in secular activities where they are to proclaim the gospel. There lacks a sense, however, that those activities themselves are ministries. Finally, as mentioned in Chapter 4, many members of the clergy are engaged in what magisterial documents classify as secular: teachers, scientists, artists, lawyers, healthcare. Doing away with the clergy-laity distinction would seem to foster greater diverse participation of all members of the church based upon their charisms rather than their state of life. Dulles writes:

> In traditional terms it is customary to speak of clergy and laity. This dichotomy can be defended, but it tends to classify everyone too narrowly with reference to ordination. More authentically Catholic, in my opinion,

is the idea that every Christian has some special gift or grace, which must be cultivated and faithfully lived out.[19]

The clergy-laity distinction may have worked well for the promotion of catholicity, and it still may work in some cultures. Applying the natural law of evolution, however, if it is no longer effective, then its usefulness has passed. As Avery Dulles observes in considering *Gaudium et spes* (no. 44), "The council makes it clear that the structures of the Church, although fundamentally given by Christ, must continually be adjusted to the times."[20] The acknowledgment that the structures of the church were not fundamentally given by Christ gives us even more flexibility in adjusting them. Dulles concludes: "The idea of a complementarity of roles, without confusion of functions, is more Catholic and more faithful to the Scriptures than the idea of unilateral subordination, with an active hierarchy dictating to a passive laity."[21]

A willingness to revise the current organization of ministry in the Catholic Church also has the potential for progress in the ecumenical movement, fostering even more the catholic identity of the church. The Vatican II *Decree on Ecumenism (Unitatis redintegratio)* teaches:

Every renewal of the Church is essentially grounded in an increase of fidelity to her own calling. Undoubtedly this is the basis of the movement toward unity.

Christ summons the Church to continual reformation as she sojourns here on earth. The Church is always in need of this, in so far as she is an institution of men here on earth. . . .

---

[19] Ibid., 125.
[20] Ibid., 101.
[21] Ibid., 126.

Church renewal has therefore notable ecumenical importance. Already in various spheres of the Church's life, this renewal is taking place. The Biblical and liturgical movements, the preaching of the word of God and catechetics, the apostolate of the laity, new forms of religious life and the spirituality of married life, and the Church's social teaching and activity—all these should be considered as pledges and signs of the future progress of ecumenism. (*UD* 6)

In 1982, the Faith and Order Commission of the World Council of Churches seems to have taken up the challenge, writing:

The Holy Spirit bestows on the community diverse and complementary gifts. These are for the common good of the whole people and are manifested in acts of service within the community and to the world. . . . All members are called to discover, with the help of the community, the gifts they have received and to use them for the building up of the Church and for the service of the world to which the Church is sent.[22]

The commission calls for the various Christian churches to forge models of ministry based upon "the calling of the whole people of God" (6). It defines ministry as "service to which the whole people of God is called, whether as individuals, as a local community, or as the universal Church. . . . *Ordained ministry* refers to persons who have received a charism and whom the church appoints for service by ordination through the invocation of the Spirit and the laying on of hands" (7). It recognizes that forms of ordained ministry have changed over the centuries and urges churches "to avoid attributing their particular forms of the ordained ministry directly to the

---

[22] WCC, "Baptism, Eucharist, Ministry," Faith and Order Paper no. 111, para. 5 (Geneva: WCC, 1982).

will and institution of Jesus Christ" (commentary 11). Among the responsibilities of the ordained ministry the commission notes the proclamation of the word, sacraments, and guiding the community. These tasks, however, are not exclusive to the ordained ministry: "Since the ordained ministry and the community are inextricably related, all members participate in fulfilling these functions. In fact, every charism serves to 'assemble and build up the body of Christ'" (commentary 13). It calls for the public recognition of the charisms of all members of the community "to enhance their effectiveness." It believes that some of these ministries can be permanent and others temporary (32).

Apostolic

The fourth mark of the church, apostolicity, can be understood in at least two related ways. On the one hand, it conveys the Christian belief that the church is founded upon and remains obedient to the faith of the first apostles. We saw earlier that specifying exactly what we mean by *apostle* isn't easy. In general, however, what theologians mean by *apostolicity* is, at least, fidelity to the faith of the first Christians. Some churches, such as the Catholic and Orthodox churches, claim that this fidelity is embodied in the unbroken succession of bishops who succeeded the first apostles. *Lumen gentium* expresses this position:

> Thus, as St. Irenaeus testifies, through those who were appointed bishops by the apostles, and through their successors down in our own time, the apostolic tradition is manifested and preserved. (*LG* 20)

The Faith and Order Commission of the World Council of Churches, on the other hand, expresses the opinion of other Christian traditions that apostolicity is guaranteed by the active presence of the Word in the church:

It is apostolic because the Word of God, sent by the Father, creates and sustains the Church. This word of God is made known to us through the Gospel primarily and normatively borne witness to by the apostles (cf. Eph 2:20; Rev 21:14), making the communion of the faithful a community that lives in, and is responsible for, the succession of the apostolic truth expressed in faith and life throughout the ages.[23]

Concern for fidelity to the faith of the first Christians, however, is not the only meaning of *apostolicity*. It also refers to Jesus's charge to the church to be apostles, people sent to proclaim the gospel. The proclamation of the gospel is a participation in the creative act of the Father who sends the Son into the world to bring creation to fulfillment by the power of the Holy Spirit. John's Gospel remembers the experience when he describes the meeting between Jesus and the disciples in a locked house, huddled in fear: "'Peace be with you.' After he said this, he showed them his hands and his side. . . . 'As the Father has sent [*apostello*] me, so I send you.'[24] When he had said this, he breathed on them and said to them, 'Receive the Holy Spirit. If you forgive [*aphiemi*] the sins of any, they are forgiven them; if you retain the sins of any, they are retained'" (John 20:21). Matthew remembers: "Go therefore and make disciples of all nations, baptizing them in the name of the Father and of the Son and of the Holy Spirit" (Matt 28:19). Luke's version is found in the Acts of the Apostles: "You will receive power when the Holy Spirit has come upon you; and

---

[23] WCC, "Nature and Mission of the Church: A Stage on the Way to a Common Statement," Faith and Order Paper no. 198, para. 12 (Geneva: WCC, 2005). See also "Baptism, Eucharist, and Ministry," para. 34.

[24] Greek uses two different verbs here for "to send," *apostello* and *pempo*. Raymond Brown thinks that there is no difference in meaning. Raymond Brown, *The Gospel according to John XIII–XXI*, Anchor Bible 29 (New Haven, CT: Yale University Press, 1970), 521.

you will be my witnesses [*martus*] in Jerusalem, in all Judea and Samaria, and to the ends of the earth" (Acts 1:8). Jesus charges us to continue the work that the Father gave him, the work of bringing creation to fulfillment. As the Father sent the Son, so the Son sends us. The Son's task is the forgiveness of sins. The verb that John uses for "forgiveness" has the sense of loosening from bonds, freeing from what constrains us. Sin constrains us from the goal for which our hearts yearn, the fulfillment to which God calls us. That goal and fulfillment are the unity, holiness, and catholicity of the Trinity. God provides us with the power and the Way to achieve that goal. As Teilhard muses, that process involves dying to selves, dying to selfishness, allowing baptism to work in us. The charge Jesus gives to the disciples in Matthew is to baptize all people into the Trinity. Baptism into the Trinity means a death to the old order of natural selection that includes selfishness and competition and a rebirth into the new order of pure altruism and cooperation, of working together. The Acts of the Apostles remembers Jesus asking the disciples to be his witnesses, which in Greek means martyrs. A witness first sees and then gives testimony. Christians see Jesus's pierced hands and his side and give testimony to the crucifixion in their own lives. There is no greater testimony than what we commonly call martyrdom, that is, dying for the faith. Many Christians have done so by being killed at the hands of other people, but all are called to do so with their lives, dying to selfishness, growing in altruism, working together.

The call to martyrdom expresses itself in *apostolates*. Apostolates are the works by which people cooperate with one another and with God. They are the ministries by which we act as co-creators with God.[25] They are how we express and live our responsibility to cultivate our humanity and to direct the evolution of the entire divine milieu toward its completion

---

[25] See further Ilia Delio, *Christ in Evolution* (Maryknoll, NY: Orbis Books, 2008), 138–55.

in its divinization. Apostolates are the means by which we use our charisms to transform what Augustine named the City of Man into the City of God. Augustine recognized that the Roman *religio* had good values that had served the Romans well in constructing their empire. From our perspective we can say that Augustine appreciated the value of the order of nature that included selfishness and altruism. But through the lens of Christian faith he also criticized the cruelty and selfishness of that nature. His conscience told him that there was a better *religio*, a better way of living; his faith told him how that was possible. It was and is possible to shed the original sin of selfishness through grace. As Ralph Wendell Burhoe proposes, *religio* "is the key and hitherto missing link in the scientific explanation of how ape-men are transformed to civilized altruism." Burhoe understands religion as "the system of rituals, myths, rational theologies, etc., that constitute and convey our basic heritage of culturally communicated values."[26] We can extend that definition to include the implementation of those values in everyday life.

Teilhard appreciates the *metánoia*, the profound conversion, which our vocation to apostolicity involves. All the work that we do, cooperating with God in evolution, constructing more and more complex open systems by using energy, is, just as importantly, the way we grow together in communion. The energy we expend on our projects draws us to shed selfishness. It loosens the bonds that divide us. It frees us from our inherited instinct to compete, to view others as competitors, to view them in some sense as enemies. It draws us into the convergence that Teilhard foresaw as he celebrated the "Mass on the World." There Teilhard writes that, not having any of the symbols available for the Eucharist, he offers "himself, your priest, on the altar of the whole Earth, the work and

---

[26] Ralph Wendell Burhoe, "Religion's Role in Human Evolution: The Missing Link between Ape-Man's Selfish Genes and Civilized Altruism," *Zygon* 14 (1979): 149; see further Keith Ferdinando, "Mission: A Problem of Definition," *Themelios* 33 (2008): 46–59.

the trouble of the World." Looking at the rising sun he meditates on the "frightening work." On his paten he places the "expected harvest of this new effort," and into his chalice he pours the "sap of all the fruits that will be crushed today." His chalice and paten are the depths of his soul that is "open to all the forces of the globe and converge toward the Spirit." All people on earth pass before his eyes: "those in their offices, laboratories, factories who believe in the progress of Things, and today passionately pursue the light." He sees people who, in their turmoil, cry out: "Lord, make us one."

Teilhard's prayer is a beautiful reflection, first upon the apostolate of Jesus, and then upon the apostolate that he confers on us. All of Jesus's works (as recorded in the New Testament) had the effect of challenging people and enabling them to respond to his initial call to *metánoia*. John's Gospel calls Jesus's miracles "signs." They not only indicated who he was—he encourages people to believe at least because they saw the signs—but they also effected, made his apostolate happen. In one form or another they brought people together, ultimately in the communion of the Eucharist. They did so through what Teilhard calls "the two hands of God": creation involves growth and diminution, or perhaps better, growth into diminution. In the *Divine Milieu* he prays: "Grant that I may begin to sketch the outline of a gesture whose full power will only be revealed to me in presence of the forces of diminishment and death."[27] The human apostolate consists of three elements, he writes: (1) collaboration for the fulfillment of creation; (2) through work grow in victory over selfishness; and (3) cherish both the wholeness and the emptiness of life. The apostolate is a sacrifice, truly a participation in the priesthood of Christ, continuing his apostolate. By exercising ministries in love, empowered by the Holy Spirit, we give ourselves away—we grow in the death that our baptism symbolizes—and we become holy by growing into the life of God who is one and catholic. Teilhard's meditation on baptism states:

---

[27] Teilhard, *The Divine Milieu*, 79.

Immersion and emergence; participation in things and sublimation; possession and renunciation; crossing through and being borne onwards—that is the twofold yet single movement which answers the challenge of matter in order to save it.[28]

The divine milieu develops only through the expression of love.[29]

Apostolicity, therefore, is how we cooperate with God as co-creators. Philip Hefner, who has developed the theory of humans as co-creators, uses both science and theology to identify the role that Homo sapiens plays in the world's evolution.[30] He explains how people have physically evolved in such a way that culture has developed:

The appearance of culture is directly correlated to the central nervous system, and the dramatic increase in the significance of culture in the human species is correlated with the equally dramatic development of the human brain. Culture is defined as learned and taught patterns of behavior, together with the symbol systems that contextualize and interpret the behavior.[31]

Hefner's definition of *culture* is how I understand *religio*. We have evolved to be "religious" in the sense that we have the possibility of organizing our lives, our activities, in function of what we perceive as our ultimate goal. For Christians, of course, that is God revealed by the Son, the fullness of whose revelation is Jesus Christ. The exercise of love expressed in work, powered by God's grace, enables us to exercise our freedom to direct evolution. Like the disciples on the road

---

[28] Ibid., 110.

[29] Ibid., 140.

[30] Philip Hefner, *The Human Factor: Evolution, Culture, and Religion* (Minneapolis: Fortress Press, 1993).

[31] Philip Hefner, "Biocultural Evolution and the Created Co-Creator," *Dialog* 36 (1997): 197.

to Emmaus, Christ appears as we share ourselves in who we are and what we do. We thereby fulfill Jesus's instructions to be his agent in baptizing the world from sin to holiness. All services, all ministries, converge in this catholic project, which contributes to the convergence of creation into Teilhard's Omega Point.

Epilogue

On a warm Sicilian December morning in 2005 I boarded a bus from Palermo to climb to the small town of Monreale in the hills above. I was in search of my cultural roots. My destination was the twelfth-century cathedral built by my distant ancestors by order of Norman King William II. As with most enterprises in Sicily, the trip took longer than I thought it would. I arrived at the doors of the great edifice just in time to see it closed for a three-hour lunch break. If I wanted to see the interior, I had no choice but to wait until four o'clock when the building would reopen. Imitating what my ancestors did, I ate lunch and studied the closed bronze cathedral doors. Events in Sicily have a way of working out, even if unexpectedly.

The bronze doors of the cathedral, crafted in 1186 by Bonanno da Pisa, also known as Pisano, mesmerized me. They are called the Doors of Paradise. They consist of forty-six squares. The eye's journey begins at the bottom of the door where one encounters two griffins and two lions, symbols of Norman Sicily. Then forty squares depict scenes from the Old Testament (the lower twenty) and the New Testament (the higher twenty). The first scenes are those of the creation of Adam and Eve, their original sin and expulsion from Eden, the drudgery of work, and more stories of human sinfulness. As the eye ascends the door we see Noah planting his vineyard, various stories of Abraham's faith, and then twelve prophets. Still rising, we are invited to contemplate the infancy narratives from Matthew's and Luke's Gospels, the baptism of Jesus followed by his temptations, the resurrection of Lazarus, the transfiguration, and then the Passion narrative, culminating in scenes of Jesus's resurrection and ascension. The left wing of the door is crowned with a larger square with an image of Mary in glory, with the inscription "Mary has ascended into heaven." The right wing portrays Jesus in glory with the inscription "I am the Light of the world." The door frame is distinctly Arabic and takes up Islamic themes present throughout the exterior of the cathedral. In the twelfth century I would have been standing in a mosaic-studded atrium intended for catechumens, that is, those preparing for baptism, and penitents preparing for readmission to full participation in the life of the community.

When four o'clock finally rolled around, the eager little crowd with whom I was waiting to enter the cathedral was finally allowed to go inside. Pisano's bronze sculptures gave forth the dazzling mosaics along the cathedral's nave, some depicting the same scenes as on the doors while others filling in with more stories from the biblical history of salvation. I looked up at the first intrado or arch at the top of which I saw concentric circles around a "black light" or "bright darkness": a symbol of divine perfection. The circles were flanked by the two archangels, Michael and Gabriel, messengers of God, who, it seemed, would accompany me in the experience of the cathedral. The medieval artists and architects were inviting me to use my imagination to synthesize the millions of tesserae, small pieces of glass and stone that formed the mosaics, in order to see beyond them to their Creator at work in creation. The mosaics depict scenes from the Old Testament starting with creation and concluding with Isaac and Jacob. The Old Testament stories conclude at the first of three barycenters or points that orbit one another. The first barycenter is located at the center of the cathedral. This probably is where the baptismal font and paschal candle had originally been situated. The second barycenter begins at the steps crowned with the first of two triumphal arches. The mosaics now depict scenes from the New Testament, starting with the birth of Jesus and the beginning of his public ministry. Two thrones are situated at the base of the second triumphal arches: one for the bishop and one for the king. The third barycenter is at the apse, the sanctuary where the altar is located. My eyes rose from the altar to the light from the single window in the sanctuary, surrounded by various saints, then to Mary holding the Christ child and flanked by angels and Peter and Paul. Finally, my eye rested at the summit on the Pantokrator, the Almighty: the Son incarnate in Christ who reveals the Father. The four evangelists are portrayed on the outer arch of the apse.

I remember this experience with awe. It was an experience of catholic ministry. My ancestors had worked together, directed by master architects and artists from at least three distinct cultures: Sicilian, Norman, and Arabic. Each contributed to the project from the richness of its cultural heritage. Imitating life—or just participating in it—the trip did not go as planned. But goodwill and persistence opened up one door even as the others were closed: an opportunity to contemplate Pisano's work. The doors, too, were the products of the collaboration of many artisans, whose work brought me together with the small crowd of people who had also arrived too late to enter the cathedral before lunch. The artwork on the doors was a tease, preparing me for the dazzling scene that awaited me inside. The panels brought together the stories of the people in the history of Israel who wrote the story of the Judeo-Christian *religio*.

After lunch the doors literally opened up to me the history of salvation, whereby I traveled down the nave of the church, so called because like a ship (*navis* in Latin) it carried me forward, drawn by the face of God. The mosaics literally mirror the catholic craftsmanship of the artisans who made them. They reflect the energy of the light in a synergistic conversion that communicated the Christian faith to me. Their work became a sacrament whereby I experienced God's salvific work in creation. The diversity of the tesserae in the mosaics was precisely what made the mosaics effective. The work propelled me forward through the nave. The symbols of the leaders of the *religio* of the workers, the thrones of the bishop and the king, oversaw the whole operation. The *religio* served as a catalyst to help me approach the mystery symbolized by the altar of sacrifice and communion. After dwelling upon that sacrament my eye perceived the light above the altar, which in turn encouraged me to look higher to Mary, mother of the church. She, the mother of God, gives birth to the Son of God, who, animated by the Holy Spirit, reveals the Father. The Father welcomes me into the communion of the Trinity and all the saints who surround the upper registers of the church.

The experience of the Cathedral of Monreale became for me an experience of the power of catholicity. Much energy was expended to organize all the tesserae, "stuff," the matter of the images of the mosaics. Thousands of workers toiled under the direction of overseers who brought together the art of diverse cultures. I, the viewer, lost control of the experience in order to be transformed by the work, the ministry, of the laborers who built the cathedral. Their catholic labor cooperated with God in producing a visual, catholic symphony of praise.

Index